Funeral Celebrant

Ceremony Planner

Veronika Sophia Robinson
Published by Starflower Press

Funeral Celebrant Ceremony Planner
Copyright Veronika Sophia Robinson
Cover photograph by Veronika Robinson
Published by Starflower Press for
Heart-led Ceremonies Celebrant Training
ISBN 978-1-7393353-4-2
March 2023

Dear Funeral Celebrant,
This planner was created to help me in my own celebrant practice of keeping essential ceremony-planning information in one place, and to support the work of our graduates at Heart-led Ceremonies Celebrant Training. I hope you find this planner augments your organisational tasks.
Veronika Robinson

Remembering the Life
of

Name   Page Number

_____

_____

_____

_____

_____

_____

_____

_____

_____

_____

_____

_____

_____

_____

_____

_____

_____

Remembering the Life
of

Name

_____

_____

_____

_____

_____

_____

_____

_____

_____

_____

_____

_____

_____

_____

_____

_____

_____

Remembering the Life
of

Name   Page Number

_____

_____

_____

_____

_____

_____

_____

_____

_____

_____

_____

_____

_____

_____

_____

_____

_____

_____

Remembering the Life
of

Name   Page Number

_____

_____

_____

_____

_____

_____

_____

_____

_____

_____

_____

_____

_____

_____

_____

_____

_____

Remembering the Life
of

Name   Page Number

_____

_____

_____

_____

_____

_____

_____

_____

_____

_____

_____

_____

_____

_____

_____

_____

_____

_____

_____

Funeral Director/Arranger:

[ ] Cremation

[ ] Burial

[ ] Memorial

Time:
Day:
Date of Ceremony:

Ceremony Venue:

Order of Service printed? Yes [ ] No [ ]
Due to Funeral Director by:

Curtain Open [ ]
Curtain Closed [ ]
Interment Music [ ]

Notes

Name of Deceased:

Date of Birth: Date of Death:
Nature of passing:

Family visit: am/pm Day: Date:

Chief mourner:

Next of kin:

Address:

Postcode:

Email:

Phone:

Other family members/friends/chief executor:

Music

Wesley [ ]   Family Supplied [ ] Organ/piano [   ]

Obitus   [ ]   Funeral Director [ ]   Other [ ]

Processional

Title_____

Singer/Composer_____

Reflection

Title_____

Singer/Composer_____

Recessional

Title_____

Singer/Composer_____

Other Music

Hymns

Prayers or Blessings:

Readings/poems:

Tribute speakers:

Ritual/s:

Donations:

Funeral Tea:

Acknowledgements:

Ashes: Interment [   ]   Scattering [   ]
Time:
Day and date:
Burial Site:

Funeral Director/Arranger:

[ ] Cremation

[ ] Burial

[ ] Memorial

Time:
Day:
Date of Ceremony:

Ceremony Venue:

Order of Service printed? Yes [ ] No [ ]
Due to Funeral Director by:

Curtain Open [ ]
Curtain Closed [ ]
Interment Music [ ]

Notes

Name of Deceased:

Date of Birth: Date of Death:
Nature of passing:

Family visit: am/pm Day: Date:

Chief mourner:

Next of kin:

Address:

Postcode:

Email:

Phone:

Other family members/friends/chief executor:

Music

Wesley [ ]   Family Supplied [ ] Organ/piano [ ]

Obitus [ ]   Funeral Director [ ] Other [ ]

Processional

Title_____

Singer/Composer_____

Reflection

Title_____

Singer/Composer_____

Recessional

Title_____

Singer/Composer_____

Other Music

Hymns

Prayers or Blessings:

Readings/poems:

Tribute speakers:

Ritual/s:

Donations:

Funeral Tea:

Acknowledgements:

Ashes: Interment [   ] Scattering [   ]
Time:
Day and date:
Burial Site:

Funeral Director/Arranger:

[ ] Cremation

[ ] Burial

[ ] Memorial

Time:
Day:
Date of Ceremony:

Ceremony Venue:

Order of Service printed? Yes [ ] No [ ]
Due to Funeral Director by:

Curtain Open [ ]
Curtain Closed [ ]
Interment Music [ ]

Notes

Name of Deceased:

Date of Birth: Date of Death:
Nature of passing:

Family visit: am/pm Day: Date:

Chief mourner:

Next of kin:

Address:

Postcode:

Email:

Phone:

Other family members/friends/chief executor:

Music

Wesley [ ]   Family Supplied [ ]   Organ/piano [ ]

Obitus [ ]   Funeral Director [ ]   Other [ ]

Processional

Title_____

Singer/Composer_____

Reflection

Title_____

Singer/Composer_____

Recessional

Title_____

Singer/Composer_____

Other Music

Hymns

Prayers or Blessings:

Readings/poems:

Tribute speakers:

Ritual/s:

Donations:

Funeral Tea:

Acknowledgements:

Ashes: Interment [ ]   Scattering [ ]
Time:
Day and date:
Burial Site:

Funeral Director/Arranger:

[ ] Cremation

[ ] Burial

[ ] Memorial

Time:
Day:
Date of Ceremony:

Ceremony Venue:

Order of Service printed? Yes [ ] No [ ]
Due to Funeral Director by:

Curtain Open [ ]
Curtain Closed [ ]
Interment Music [ ]

Notes

Name of Deceased:

Date of Birth: Date of Death:
Nature of passing:

Family visit: am/pm Day: Date:

Chief mourner:

Next of kin:

Address:

Postcode:

Email:

Phone:

Other family members/friends/chief executor:

Music

Wesley [ ]   Family Supplied [ ] Organ/piano [   ]

Obitus   [ ]   Funeral Director [   ] Other [ ]

Processional

Title_____

Singer/Composer_____

Reflection

Title_____

Singer/Composer_____

Recessional

Title_____

Singer/Composer_____

Other Music

Hymns

Prayers or Blessings:

Readings/poems:

Tribute speakers:

Ritual/s:

Donations:

Funeral Tea:

Acknowledgements:

Ashes: Interment [   ]   Scattering [   ]
Time:
Day and date:
Burial Site:

Funeral Director/Arranger:

[ ] Cremation

[ ] Burial

[ ] Memorial

Time:
Day:
Date of Ceremony:

Ceremony Venue:

Order of Service printed? Yes [ ] No [ ]
Due to Funeral Director by:

Curtain Open [ ]
Curtain Closed [ ]
Interment Music [ ]

Notes

Name of Deceased:

Date of Birth: Date of Death:
Nature of passing:

Family visit: am/pm Day: Date:

Chief mourner:

Next of kin:

Address:

Postcode:

Email:

Phone:

Other family members/friends/chief executor:

Music

Wesley [ ]   Family Supplied [ ] Organ/piano [ ]

Obitus [ ]   Funeral Director [ ] Other [ ]

Processional

Title_____

Singer/Composer_____

Reflection

Title_____

Singer/Composer_____

Recessional

Title_____

Singer/Composer_____

Other Music

Hymns

Prayers or Blessings:

Readings/poems:

Tribute speakers:

Ritual/s:

Donations:

Funeral Tea:

Acknowledgements:

Ashes: Interment [ ] Scattering [ ]
Time:
Day and date:
Burial Site:

Funeral Director/Arranger:

[ ] Cremation

[ ] Burial

[ ] Memorial

Time:
Day:
Date of Ceremony:

Ceremony Venue:

Order of Service printed? Yes [ ] No [ ]
Due to Funeral Director by:

Curtain Open [ ]
Curtain Closed [ ]
Interment Music [ ]

Notes

Name of Deceased:

Date of Birth: Date of Death:
Nature of passing:

Family visit: am/pm Day: Date:

Chief mourner:

Next of kin:

Address:

Postcode:

Email:

Phone:

Other family members/friends/chief executor:

Music

Wesley [ ]   Family Supplied [ ] Organ/piano [ ]

Obitus [ ]   Funeral Director [ ] Other [ ]

Processional

Title_____

Singer/Composer_____

Reflection

Title_____

Singer/Composer_____

Recessional

Title_____

Singer/Composer_____

Other Music

Hymns

Prayers or Blessings:

Readings/poems:

Tribute speakers:

Ritual/s:

Donations:

Funeral Tea:

Acknowledgements:

Ashes: Interment [ ] Scattering [ ]
Time:
Day and date:
Burial Site:

Funeral Director/Arranger:

[ ] Cremation

[ ] Burial

[ ] Memorial

Time:
Day:
Date of Ceremony:

Ceremony Venue:

Order of Service printed? Yes [ ] No [ ]
Due to Funeral Director by:

Curtain Open [ ]
Curtain Closed [ ]
Interment Music [ ]

Notes

Name of Deceased:

Date of Birth: Date of Death:
Nature of passing:

Family visit: am/pm Day: Date:

Chief mourner:

Next of kin:

Address:

Postcode:

Email:

Phone:

Other family members/friends/chief executor:

Music

Wesley [ ]   Family Supplied [ ] Organ/piano [ ]

Obitus [ ]   Funeral Director [ ] Other [ ]

Processional

Title_____

Singer/Composer_____

Reflection

Title_____

Singer/Composer_____

Recessional

Title_____

Singer/Composer_____

Other Music

Hymns

Prayers or Blessings:

Readings/poems:

Tribute speakers:

Ritual/s:

Donations:

Funeral Tea:

Acknowledgements:

Ashes: Interment [   ] Scattering [   ]
Time:
Day and date:
Burial Site:

Funeral Director/Arranger:

[ ] Cremation

[ ] Burial

[ ] Memorial

Time:
Day:
Date of Ceremony:

Ceremony Venue:

Order of Service printed? Yes [ ] No [ ]
Due to Funeral Director by:

Curtain Open [ ]
Curtain Closed [ ]
Interment Music [ ]

Notes

Name of Deceased:

Date of Birth: Date of Death:
Nature of passing:

Family visit: am/pm Day: Date:

Chief mourner:

Next of kin:

Address:

Postcode:

Email:

Phone:

Other family members/friends/chief executor:

Music

Wesley [ ]   Family Supplied [ ] Organ/piano [   ]

Obitus   [ ]   Funeral Director [ ] Other [ ]

Processional

Title_____

Singer/Composer_____

Reflection

Title_____

Singer/Composer_____

Recessional

Title_____

Singer/Composer_____

Other Music

Hymns

Prayers or Blessings:

Readings/poems:

Tribute speakers:

Ritual/s:

Donations:

Funeral Tea:

Acknowledgements:

Ashes: Interment [   ] Scattering [   ]
Time:
Day and date:
Burial Site:

Funeral Director/Arranger:

[ ] Cremation

[ ] Burial

[ ] Memorial

Time:
Day:
Date of Ceremony:

Ceremony Venue:

Order of Service printed? Yes [ ] No [ ]
Due to Funeral Director by:

Curtain Open [ ]
Curtain Closed [ ]
Interment Music [ ]

Notes

Name of Deceased:

Date of Birth: Date of Death:
Nature of passing:

Family visit: am/pm Day: Date:

Chief mourner:

Next of kin:

Address:

Postcode:

Email:

Phone:

Other family members/friends/chief executor:

Music

Wesley [ ]   Family Supplied [ ] Organ/piano [ ]

Obitus [ ]   Funeral Director [ ] Other [ ]

Processional

Title_____

Singer/Composer_____

Reflection

Title_____

Singer/Composer_____

Recessional

Title_____

Singer/Composer_____

Other Music

Hymns

Prayers or Blessings:

Readings/poems:

Tribute speakers:

Ritual/s:

Donations:

Funeral Tea:

Acknowledgements:

Ashes: Interment [ ] Scattering [ ]
Time:
Day and date:
Burial Site:

Funeral Director/Arranger:

[ ] Cremation

[ ] Burial

[ ] Memorial

Time:
Day:
Date of Ceremony:

Ceremony Venue:

Order of Service printed? Yes [ ] No [ ]
Due to Funeral Director by:

Curtain Open [ ]
Curtain Closed [ ]
Interment Music [ ]

Notes

Name of Deceased:

Date of Birth: Date of Death:
Nature of passing:

Family visit: am/pm Day: Date:

Chief mourner:

Next of kin:

Address:

Postcode:

Email:

Phone:

Other family members/friends/chief executor:

Music

Wesley [ ]   Family Supplied [ ] Organ/piano [   ]

Obitus [ ]   Funeral Director [ ] Other [ ]

Processional

Title_____

Singer/Composer_____

Reflection

Title_____

Singer/Composer_____

Recessional

Title_____

Singer/Composer_____

Other Music

Hymns

Prayers or Blessings:

Readings/poems:

Tribute speakers:

Ritual/s:

Donations:

Funeral Tea:

Acknowledgements:

Ashes: Interment [   ]   Scattering [   ]
Time:
Day and date:
Burial Site:

Funeral Director/Arranger:

[ ] Cremation

[ ] Burial

[ ] Memorial

Time:
Day:
Date of Ceremony:

Ceremony Venue:

Order of Service printed? Yes [ ] No [ ]
Due to Funeral Director by:

Curtain Open [ ]
Curtain Closed [ ]
Interment Music [ ]

Notes

Name of Deceased:

Date of Birth: Date of Death:
Nature of passing:

Family visit: am/pm Day: Date:

Chief mourner:

Next of kin:

Address:

Postcode:

Email:

Phone:

Other family members/friends/chief executor:

Music

Wesley [ ]   Family Supplied [ ] Organ/piano [ ]

Obitus [ ]   Funeral Director [ ] Other [ ]

Processional

Title_____

Singer/Composer_____

Reflection

Title_____

Singer/Composer_____

Recessional

Title_____

Singer/Composer_____

Other Music

Hymns

Prayers or Blessings:

Readings/poems:

Tribute speakers:

Ritual/s:

Donations:

Funeral Tea:

Acknowledgements:

Ashes: Interment [ ] Scattering [ ]
Time:
Day and date:
Burial Site:

Funeral Director/Arranger:

[ ] Cremation

[ ] Burial

[ ] Memorial

Time:
Day:
Date of Ceremony:

Ceremony Venue:

Order of Service printed? Yes [ ] No [ ]
Due to Funeral Director by:

Curtain Open [ ]
Curtain Closed [ ]
Interment Music [ ]

Notes

Name of Deceased:

Date of Birth: Date of Death:
Nature of passing:

Family visit: am/pm Day: Date:

Chief mourner:

Next of kin:

Address:

Postcode:

Email:

Phone:

Other family members/friends/chief executor:

Music

Wesley [ ]   Family Supplied [ ] Organ/piano [ ]

Obitus   [ ]   Funeral Director [ ]   Other [ ]

Processional

Title_____

Singer/Composer_____

Reflection

Title_____

Singer/Composer_____

Recessional

Title_____

Singer/Composer_____

Other Music

Hymns

Prayers or Blessings:

Readings/poems:

Tribute speakers:

Ritual/s:

Donations:

Funeral Tea:

Acknowledgements:

Ashes: Interment [   ]   Scattering [ ]
Time:
Day and date:
Burial Site:

Funeral Director/Arranger:

[ ] Cremation

[ ] Burial

[ ] Memorial

Time:
Day:
Date of Ceremony:

Ceremony Venue:

Order of Service printed? Yes [ ] No [ ]
Due to Funeral Director by:

Curtain Open [ ]
Curtain Closed [ ]
Interment Music [ ]

Notes

Name of Deceased:

Date of Birth: Date of Death:
Nature of passing:

Family visit: am/pm Day: Date:

Chief mourner:

Next of kin:

Address:

Postcode:

Email:

Phone:

Other family members/friends/chief executor:

Music

Wesley [ ]   Family Supplied [ ] Organ/piano [ ]

Obitus   [ ]   Funeral Director [ ] Other [ ]

Processional

Title_____

Singer/Composer_____

Reflection

Title_____

Singer/Composer_____

Recessional

Title_____

Singer/Composer_____

Other Music

Hymns

Prayers or Blessings:

Readings/poems:

Tribute speakers:

Ritual/s:

Donations:

Funeral Tea:

Acknowledgements:

Ashes: Interment [ ] Scattering [ ]
Time:
Day and date:
Burial Site:

Funeral Director/Arranger:

[ ] Cremation

[ ] Burial

[ ] Memorial

Time:
Day:
Date of Ceremony:

Ceremony Venue:

Order of Service printed? Yes [ ] No [ ]
Due to Funeral Director by:

Curtain Open [ ]
Curtain Closed [ ]
Interment Music [ ]

Notes

Name of Deceased:

Date of Birth: Date of Death:
Nature of passing:

Family visit: am/pm Day: Date:

Chief mourner:

Next of kin:

Address:

Postcode:

Email:

Phone:

Other family members/friends/chief executor:

Music

Wesley [ ]   Family Supplied [ ] Organ/piano [   ]

Obitus   [ ]   Funeral Director [ ]   Other [ ]

Processional

Title_____

Singer/Composer_____

Reflection

Title_____

Singer/Composer_____

Recessional

Title_____

Singer/Composer_____

Other Music

Hymns

Prayers or Blessings:

Readings/poems:

Tribute speakers:

Ritual/s:

Donations:

Funeral Tea:

Acknowledgements:

Ashes: Interment [   ]   Scattering [   ]
Time:
Day and date:
Burial Site:

Funeral Director/Arranger:

[ ] Cremation

[ ] Burial

[ ] Memorial

Time:
Day:
Date of Ceremony:

Ceremony Venue:

Order of Service printed? Yes [ ] No [ ]
Due to Funeral Director by:

Curtain Open [ ]
Curtain Closed [ ]
Interment Music [ ]

Notes

Name of Deceased:

Date of Birth: Date of Death:
Nature of passing:

Family visit: am/pm Day: Date:

Chief mourner:

Next of kin:

Address:

Postcode:

Email:

Phone:

Other family members/friends/chief executor:

Music

Wesley [ ]   Family Supplied [ ] Organ/piano [   ]

Obitus [ ]   Funeral Director [ ]   Other [ ]

Processional

Title_____

Singer/Composer_____

Reflection

Title_____

Singer/Composer_____

Recessional

Title_____

Singer/Composer_____

Other Music

Hymns

Prayers or Blessings:

Readings/poems:

Tribute speakers:

Ritual/s:

Donations:

Funeral Tea:

Acknowledgements:

Ashes: Interment [   ]   Scattering [   ]
Time:
Day and date:
Burial Site:

Funeral Director/Arranger:

[ ] Cremation

[ ] Burial

[ ] Memorial

Time:
Day:
Date of Ceremony:

Ceremony Venue:

Order of Service printed? Yes [ ] No [ ]
Due to Funeral Director by:

Curtain Open [ ]
Curtain Closed [ ]
Interment Music [ ]

Notes

Name of Deceased:

Date of Birth: Date of Death:
Nature of passing:

Family visit: am/pm Day: Date:

Chief mourner:

Next of kin:

Address:

Postcode:

Email:

Phone:

Other family members/friends/chief executor:

Music

Wesley [ ]   Family Supplied [ ] Organ/piano [ ]

Obitus [ ]   Funeral Director [ ] Other [ ]

Processional

Title_____

Singer/Composer_____

Reflection

Title_____

Singer/Composer_____

Recessional

Title_____

Singer/Composer_____

Other Music

Hymns

Prayers or Blessings:

Readings/poems:

Tribute speakers:

Ritual/s:

Donations:

Funeral Tea:

Acknowledgements:

Ashes: Interment [ ]   Scattering [ ]
Time:
Day and date:
Burial Site:

Funeral Director/Arranger:

[ ] Cremation

[ ] Burial

[ ] Memorial

Time:
Day:
Date of Ceremony:

Ceremony Venue:

Order of Service printed? Yes [ ] No [ ]
Due to Funeral Director by:

Curtain Open [ ]
Curtain Closed [ ]
Interment Music [ ]

Notes

Name of Deceased:

Date of Birth: Date of Death:
Nature of passing:

Family visit: am/pm Day: Date:

Chief mourner:

Next of kin:

Address:

Postcode:

Email:

Phone:

Other family members/friends/chief executor:

Music

Wesley [ ]   Family Supplied [ ] Organ/piano [ ]

Obitus [ ]   Funeral Director [ ] Other [ ]

Processional

Title_____

Singer/Composer_____

Reflection

Title_____

Singer/Composer_____

Recessional

Title_____

Singer/Composer_____

Other Music

Hymns

Prayers or Blessings:

Readings/poems:

Tribute speakers:

Ritual/s:

Donations:

Funeral Tea:

Acknowledgements:

Ashes: Interment [ ] Scattering [ ]
Time:
Day and date:
Burial Site:

Funeral Director/Arranger:

[ ] Cremation

[ ] Burial

[ ] Memorial

Time:
Day:
Date of Ceremony:

Ceremony Venue:

Order of Service printed? Yes [ ] No [ ]
Due to Funeral Director by:

Curtain Open [ ]
Curtain Closed [ ]
Interment Music [ ]

Notes

Name of Deceased:

Date of Birth: Date of Death:
Nature of passing:

Family visit: am/pm Day: Date:

Chief mourner:

Next of kin:

Address:

Postcode:

Email:

Phone:

Other family members/friends/chief executor:

Music

Wesley [ ]　　　　Family Supplied [ ] Organ/piano [ ]

Obitus [ ]　　　　Funeral Director [ ]　Other [ ]

Processional

Title_____

Singer/Composer_____

Reflection

Title_____

Singer/Composer_____

Recessional

Title_____

Singer/Composer_____

Other Music

Hymns

Prayers or Blessings:

Readings/poems:

Tribute speakers:

Ritual/s:

Donations:

Funeral Tea:

Acknowledgements:

Ashes: Interment [　]　Scattering [　]
Time:
Day and date:
Burial Site:

Funeral Director/Arranger:

[ ] Cremation

[ ] Burial

[ ] Memorial

Time:
Day:
Date of Ceremony:

Ceremony Venue:

Order of Service printed? Yes [ ] No [ ]
Due to Funeral Director by:

Curtain Open [ ]
Curtain Closed [ ]
Interment Music [ ]

Notes

Name of Deceased:

Date of Birth: Date of Death:
Nature of passing:

Family visit: am/pm Day: Date:

Chief mourner:

Next of kin:

Address:

Postcode:

Email:

Phone:

Other family members/friends/chief executor:

Music

Wesley [ ]   Family Supplied [ ] Organ/piano [   ]

Obitus   [ ]   Funeral Director [ ] Other [ ]

Processional

Title_____

Singer/Composer_____

Reflection

Title_____

Singer/Composer_____

Recessional

Title_____

Singer/Composer_____

Other Music

Hymns

Prayers or Blessings:

Readings/poems:

Tribute speakers:

Ritual/s:

Donations:

Funeral Tea:

Acknowledgements:

Ashes: Interment [   ]   Scattering [   ]
Time:
Day and date:
Burial Site:

Funeral Director/Arranger:

[ ] Cremation

[ ] Burial

[ ] Memorial

Time:
Day:
Date of Ceremony:

Ceremony Venue:

Order of Service printed? Yes [ ] No [ ]
Due to Funeral Director by:

Curtain Open [ ]
Curtain Closed [ ]
Interment Music [ ]

Notes

Name of Deceased:

Date of Birth: Date of Death:
Nature of passing:

Family visit: am/pm Day: Date:

Chief mourner:

Next of kin:

Address:

Postcode:

Email:

Phone:

Other family members/friends/chief executor:

Music

Wesley [ ]   Family Supplied [ ] Organ/piano [ ]

Obitus   [ ]   Funeral Director [ ] Other [ ]

Processional

Title_____

Singer/Composer_____

Reflection

Title_____

Singer/Composer_____

Recessional

Title_____

Singer/Composer_____

Other Music

Hymns

Prayers or Blessings:

Readings/poems:

Tribute speakers:

Ritual/s:

Donations:

Funeral Tea:

Acknowledgements:

Ashes: Interment [   ] Scattering [   ]
Time:
Day and date:
Burial Site:

Funeral Director/Arranger:

[ ] Cremation

[ ] Burial

[ ] Memorial

Time:
Day:
Date of Ceremony:

Ceremony Venue:

Order of Service printed? Yes [ ] No [ ]
Due to Funeral Director by:

Curtain Open [ ]
Curtain Closed [ ]
Interment Music [ ]

Notes

Name of Deceased:

Date of Birth: Date of Death:
Nature of passing:

Family visit: am/pm Day: Date:

Chief mourner:

Next of kin:

Address:

Postcode:

Email:

Phone:

Other family members/friends/chief executor:

Music

Wesley [ ]   Family Supplied [ ] Organ/piano [   ]

Obitus [ ]   Funeral Director [ ] Other [ ]

Processional

Title_____

Singer/Composer_____

Reflection

Title_____

Singer/Composer_____

Recessional

Title_____

Singer/Composer_____

Other Music

Hymns

Prayers or Blessings:

Readings/poems:

Tribute speakers:

Ritual/s:

Donations:

Funeral Tea:

Acknowledgements:

Ashes: Interment [   ]   Scattering [   ]
Time:
Day and date:
Burial Site:

Funeral Director/Arranger:

[ ] Cremation

[ ] Burial

[ ] Memorial

Time:
Day:
Date of Ceremony:

Ceremony Venue:

Order of Service printed? Yes [ ] No [ ]
Due to Funeral Director by:

Curtain Open [ ]
Curtain Closed [ ]
Interment Music [ ]

Notes

Name of Deceased:

Date of Birth: Date of Death:
Nature of passing:

Family visit: am/pm Day: Date:

Chief mourner:

Next of kin:

Address:

Postcode:

Email:

Phone:

Other family members/friends/chief executor:

Music

Wesley [ ]   Family Supplied [ ] Organ/piano [ ]

Obitus [ ]   Funeral Director [ ] Other [ ]

Processional

Title_____

Singer/Composer_____

Reflection

Title_____

Singer/Composer_____

Recessional

Title_____

Singer/Composer_____

Other Music

Hymns

Prayers or Blessings:

Readings/poems:

Tribute speakers:

Ritual/s:

Donations:

Funeral Tea:

Acknowledgements:

Ashes: Interment [ ] Scattering [ ]
Time:
Day and date:
Burial Site:

Funeral Director/Arranger:

[ ] Cremation

[ ] Burial

[ ] Memorial

Time:
Day:
Date of Ceremony:

Ceremony Venue:

Order of Service printed? Yes [ ] No [ ]
Due to Funeral Director by:

Curtain Open [ ]
Curtain Closed [ ]
Interment Music [ ]

Notes

Name of Deceased:

Date of Birth: Date of Death:
Nature of passing:

Family visit: am/pm Day: Date:

Chief mourner:

Next of kin:

Address:

Postcode:

Email:

Phone:

Other family members/friends/chief executor:

Music

Wesley [ ]   Family Supplied [ ] Organ/piano [ ]

Obitus [ ]   Funeral Director [ ] Other [ ]

Processional

Title_____

Singer/Composer_____

Reflection

Title_____

Singer/Composer_____

Recessional

Title_____

Singer/Composer_____

Other Music

Hymns

Prayers or Blessings:

Readings/poems:

Tribute speakers:

Ritual/s:

Donations:

Funeral Tea:

Acknowledgements:

Ashes: Interment [   ]   Scattering [   ]
Time:
Day and date:
Burial Site:

Funeral Director/Arranger:

[ ] Cremation

[ ] Burial

[ ] Memorial

Time:
Day:
Date of Ceremony:

Ceremony Venue:

Order of Service printed? Yes [ ] No [ ]
Due to Funeral Director by:

Curtain Open [ ]
Curtain Closed [ ]
Interment Music [ ]

Notes

Name of Deceased:

Date of Birth: Date of Death:
Nature of passing:

Family visit: am/pm Day: Date:

Chief mourner:

Next of kin:

Address:

Postcode:

Email:

Phone:

Other family members/friends/chief executor:

Music

Wesley [ ]　　　Family Supplied [ ] Organ/piano [　]

Obitus　[ ]　　　Funeral Director [ ] Other [ ]

Processional

Title_____

Singer/Composer_____

Reflection

Title_____

Singer/Composer_____

Recessional

Title_____

Singer/Composer_____

Other Music

Hymns

Prayers or Blessings:

Readings/poems:

Tribute speakers:

Ritual/s:

Donations:

Funeral Tea:

Acknowledgements:

Ashes: Interment [　]　Scattering [　]
Time:
Day and date:
Burial Site:

Funeral Director/Arranger:

[ ] Cremation

[ ] Burial

[ ] Memorial

Time:
Day:
Date of Ceremony:

Ceremony Venue:

Order of Service printed? Yes [ ] No [ ]
Due to Funeral Director by:

Curtain Open [ ]
Curtain Closed [ ]
Interment Music [ ]

Notes

Name of Deceased:

Date of Birth: Date of Death:
Nature of passing:

Family visit: am/pm Day: Date:

Chief mourner:

Next of kin:

Address:

Postcode:

Email:

Phone:

Other family members/friends/chief executor:

Music

Wesley [ ]   Family Supplied [ ] Organ/piano [   ]

Obitus   [ ]   Funeral Director [ ]   Other [ ]

Processional

Title_____

Singer/Composer_____

Reflection

Title_____

Singer/Composer_____

Recessional

Title_____

Singer/Composer_____

Other Music

Hymns

Prayers or Blessings:

Readings/poems:

Tribute speakers:

Ritual/s:

Donations:

Funeral Tea:

Acknowledgements:

Ashes: Interment [   ]   Scattering [   ]
Time:
Day and date:
Burial Site:

Funeral Director/Arranger:

[ ] Cremation

[ ] Burial

[ ] Memorial

Time:
Day:
Date of Ceremony:

Ceremony Venue:

Order of Service printed? Yes [ ] No [ ]
Due to Funeral Director by:

Curtain Open [ ]
Curtain Closed [ ]
Interment Music [ ]

Notes

Name of Deceased:

Date of Birth: Date of Death:
Nature of passing:

Family visit: am/pm Day: Date:

Chief mourner:

Next of kin:

Address:

Postcode:

Email:

Phone:

Other family members/friends/chief executor:

Music

Wesley [ ]   Family Supplied [ ] Organ/piano [ ]

Obitus [ ]   Funeral Director [ ] Other [ ]

Processional

Title_____

Singer/Composer_____

Reflection

Title_____

Singer/Composer_____

Recessional

Title_____

Singer/Composer_____

Other Music

Hymns

Prayers or Blessings:

Readings/poems:

Tribute speakers:

Ritual/s:

Donations:

Funeral Tea:

Acknowledgements:

Ashes: Interment [ ] Scattering [ ]
Time:
Day and date:
Burial Site:

Funeral Director/Arranger:

[ ] Cremation

[ ] Burial

[ ] Memorial

Time:
Day:
Date of Ceremony:

Ceremony Venue:

Order of Service printed? Yes [ ] No [ ]
Due to Funeral Director by:

Curtain Open [ ]
Curtain Closed [ ]
Interment Music [ ]

Notes

Name of Deceased:

Date of Birth: Date of Death:
Nature of passing:

Family visit: am/pm Day: Date:

Chief mourner:

Next of kin:

Address:

Postcode:

Email:

Phone:

Other family members/friends/chief executor:

Music

Wesley [ ]   Family Supplied [ ] Organ/piano [   ]

Obitus [ ]   Funeral Director [ ]   Other [ ]

Processional

Title_____

Singer/Composer_____

Reflection

Title_____

Singer/Composer_____

Recessional

Title_____

Singer/Composer_____

Other Music

Hymns

Prayers or Blessings:

Readings/poems:

Tribute speakers:

Ritual/s:

Donations:

Funeral Tea:

Acknowledgements:

Ashes: Interment [   ] Scattering [   ]
Time:
Day and date:
Burial Site:

Funeral Director/Arranger:

[ ] Cremation

[ ] Burial

[ ] Memorial

Time:
Day:
Date of Ceremony:

Ceremony Venue:

Order of Service printed? Yes [ ] No [ ]
Due to Funeral Director by:

Curtain Open [ ]
Curtain Closed [ ]
Interment Music [ ]

Notes

Name of Deceased:

Date of Birth: Date of Death:
Nature of passing:

Family visit: am/pm Day: Date:

Chief mourner:

Next of kin:

Address:

Postcode:

Email:

Phone:

Other family members/friends/chief executor:

Music

Wesley [ ]   Family Supplied [ ] Organ/piano [ ]

Obitus [ ]   Funeral Director [ ] Other [ ]

Processional

Title_____

Singer/Composer_____

Reflection

Title_____

Singer/Composer_____

Recessional

Title_____

Singer/Composer_____

Other Music

Hymns

Prayers or Blessings:

Readings/poems:

Tribute speakers:

Ritual/s:

Donations:

Funeral Tea:

Acknowledgements:

Ashes: Interment [ ] Scattering [ ]
Time:
Day and date:
Burial Site:

Funeral Director/Arranger:

[ ] Cremation

[ ] Burial

[ ] Memorial

Time:
Day:
Date of Ceremony:

Ceremony Venue:

Order of Service printed? Yes [ ] No [ ]
Due to Funeral Director by:

Curtain Open [ ]
Curtain Closed [ ]
Interment Music [ ]

Notes

Name of Deceased:

Date of Birth: Date of Death:
Nature of passing:

Family visit: am/pm Day: Date:

Chief mourner:

Next of kin:

Address:

Postcode:

Email:

Phone:

Other family members/friends/chief executor:

Music

Wesley [ ]   Family Supplied [ ] Organ/piano [ ]

Obitus [ ]   Funeral Director [ ]   Other [ ]

Processional

Title_____

Singer/Composer_____

Reflection

Title_____

Singer/Composer_____

Recessional

Title_____

Singer/Composer_____

Other Music

Hymns

Prayers or Blessings:

Readings/poems:

Tribute speakers:

Ritual/s:

Donations:

Funeral Tea:

Acknowledgements:

Ashes: Interment [ ] Scattering [ ]
Time:
Day and date:
Burial Site:

Funeral Director/Arranger:

[ ] Cremation

[ ] Burial

[ ] Memorial

Time:
Day:
Date of Ceremony:

Ceremony Venue:

Order of Service printed? Yes [ ] No [ ]
Due to Funeral Director by:

Curtain Open [ ]
Curtain Closed [ ]
Interment Music [ ]

Notes

Name of Deceased:

Date of Birth: Date of Death:
Nature of passing:

Family visit: am/pm Day: Date:

Chief mourner:

Next of kin:

Address:

Postcode:

Email:

Phone:

Other family members/friends/chief executor:

Music

Wesley [ ]   Family Supplied [ ] Organ/piano [   ]

Obitus   [ ]   Funeral Director [ ]   Other [ ]

Processional

Title_____

Singer/Composer_____

Reflection

Title_____

Singer/Composer_____

Recessional

Title_____

Singer/Composer_____

Other Music

Hymns

Prayers or Blessings:

Readings/poems:

Tribute speakers:

Ritual/s:

Donations:

Funeral Tea:

Acknowledgements:

Ashes: Interment [   ]   Scattering [   ]
Time:
Day and date:
Burial Site:

```
Funeral Director/Arranger:

[ ] Cremation

[ ] Burial

[ ] Memorial

Time:
Day:
Date of Ceremony:

Ceremony Venue:


Order of Service printed? Yes [ ]  No [ ]
Due to Funeral Director by:
```

Curtain Open [ ]
Curtain Closed [ ]
Interment Music [ ]

Notes

Name of Deceased:

Date of Birth: Date of Death:
Nature of passing:

Family visit: am/pm Day: Date:

Chief mourner:

Next of kin:

Address:

Postcode:

Email:

Phone:

Other family members/friends/chief executor:

Music

Wesley [ ]   Family Supplied [ ] Organ/piano [ ]

Obitus   [ ]   Funeral Director [ ]   Other [ ]

Processional

Title_____

Singer/Composer_____

Reflection

Title_____

Singer/Composer_____

Recessional

Title_____

Singer/Composer_____

Other Music

Hymns

Prayers or Blessings:

Readings/poems:

Tribute speakers:

Ritual/s:

Donations:

Funeral Tea:

Acknowledgements:

Ashes: Interment [ ] Scattering [ ]
Time:
Day and date:
Burial Site:

Funeral Director/Arranger:

[ ] Cremation

[ ] Burial

[ ] Memorial

Time:
Day:
Date of Ceremony:

Ceremony Venue:

Order of Service printed? Yes [ ] No [ ]
Due to Funeral Director by:

Curtain Open [ ]
Curtain Closed [ ]
Interment Music [ ]

Notes

Name of Deceased:

Date of Birth: Date of Death:
Nature of passing:

Family visit: am/pm Day: Date:

Chief mourner:

Next of kin:

Address:

Postcode:

Email:

Phone:

Other family members/friends/chief executor:

Music

Wesley [ ]   Family Supplied [ ] Organ/piano [   ]

Obitus   [ ]   Funeral Director [ ] Other [ ]

Processional

Title_____

Singer/Composer_____

Reflection

Title_____

Singer/Composer_____

Recessional

Title_____

Singer/Composer_____

Other Music

Hymns

Prayers or Blessings:

Readings/poems:

Tribute speakers:

Ritual/s:

Donations:

Funeral Tea:

Acknowledgements:

Ashes: Interment [   ]   Scattering [   ]
Time:
Day and date:
Burial Site:

Funeral Director/Arranger:

[ ] Cremation

[ ] Burial

[ ] Memorial

Time:
Day:
Date of Ceremony:

Ceremony Venue:

Order of Service printed? Yes [ ] No [ ]
Due to Funeral Director by:

Curtain Open [ ]
Curtain Closed [ ]
Interment Music [ ]

Notes

Name of Deceased:

Date of Birth: Date of Death:
Nature of passing:

Family visit: am/pm Day: Date:

Chief mourner:

Next of kin:

Address:

Postcode:

Email:

Phone:

Other family members/friends/chief executor:

Music

Wesley [ ]   Family Supplied [ ] Organ/piano [   ]

Obitus   [ ]   Funeral Director [ ] Other [ ]

Processional

Title_____

Singer/Composer_____

Reflection

Title_____

Singer/Composer_____

Recessional

Title_____

Singer/Composer_____

Other Music

Hymns

Prayers or Blessings:

Readings/poems:

Tribute speakers:

Ritual/s:

Donations:

Funeral Tea:

Acknowledgements:

Ashes: Interment [   ] Scattering [   ]
Time:
Day and date:
Burial Site:

Funeral Director/Arranger:

[ ] Cremation

[ ] Burial

[ ] Memorial

Time:
Day:
Date of Ceremony:

Ceremony Venue:

Order of Service printed? Yes [ ] No [ ]
Due to Funeral Director by:

Curtain Open [ ]
Curtain Closed [ ]
Interment Music [ ]

Notes

Name of Deceased:

Date of Birth: Date of Death:
Nature of passing:

Family visit: am/pm Day: Date:

Chief mourner:

Next of kin:

Address:

Postcode:

Email:

Phone:

Other family members/friends/chief executor:

Music

Wesley [ ]   Family Supplied [ ] Organ/piano [   ]

Obitus   [ ]   Funeral Director [ ]   Other [   ]

Processional

Title_____

Singer/Composer_____

Reflection

Title_____

Singer/Composer_____

Recessional

Title_____

Singer/Composer_____

Other Music

Hymns

Prayers or Blessings:

Readings/poems:

Tribute speakers:

Ritual/s:

Donations:

Funeral Tea:

Acknowledgements:

Ashes: Interment [   ]   Scattering [   ]
Time:
Day and date:
Burial Site:

Funeral Director/Arranger:

[ ] Cremation

[ ] Burial

[ ] Memorial

Time:
Day:
Date of Ceremony:

Ceremony Venue:

Order of Service printed? Yes [ ] No [ ]
Due to Funeral Director by:

Curtain Open [ ]
Curtain Closed [ ]
Interment Music [ ]

Notes

Name of Deceased:

Date of Birth: Date of Death:
Nature of passing:

Family visit: am/pm Day: Date:

Chief mourner:

Next of kin:

Address:

Postcode:

Email:

Phone:

Other family members/friends/chief executor:

Music

Wesley [ ]   Family Supplied [ ] Organ/piano [   ]

Obitus   [ ]   Funeral Director [ ]   Other [ ]

Processional

Title_____

Singer/Composer_____

Reflection

Title_____

Singer/Composer_____

Recessional

Title_____

Singer/Composer_____

Other Music

Hymns

Prayers or Blessings:

Readings/poems:

Tribute speakers:

Ritual/s:

Donations:

Funeral Tea:

Acknowledgements:

Ashes: Interment [   ]   Scattering [   ]
Time:
Day and date:
Burial Site:

Funeral Director/Arranger:

[ ] Cremation

[ ] Burial

[ ] Memorial

Time:
Day:
Date of Ceremony:

Ceremony Venue:

Order of Service printed? Yes [ ] No [ ]
Due to Funeral Director by:

Curtain Open [ ]
Curtain Closed [ ]
Interment Music [ ]

Notes

Name of Deceased:

Date of Birth: Date of Death:
Nature of passing:

Family visit: am/pm Day: Date:

Chief mourner:

Next of kin:

Address:

Postcode:

Email:

Phone:

Other family members/friends/chief executor:

Music

Wesley [ ]   Family Supplied [ ] Organ/piano [   ]

Obitus   [ ]   Funeral Director [ ]   Other [ ]

Processional

Title_____

Singer/Composer_____

Reflection

Title_____

Singer/Composer_____

Recessional

Title_____

Singer/Composer_____

Other Music

Hymns

Prayers or Blessings:

Readings/poems:

Tribute speakers:

Ritual/s:

Donations:

Funeral Tea:

Acknowledgements:

Ashes: Interment [   ]   Scattering [   ]
Time:
Day and date:
Burial Site:

Funeral Director/Arranger:

[ ] Cremation

[ ] Burial

[ ] Memorial

Time:
Day:
Date of Ceremony:

Ceremony Venue:

Order of Service printed? Yes [ ] No [ ]
Due to Funeral Director by:

Curtain Open [ ]
Curtain Closed [ ]
Interment Music [ ]

Notes

Name of Deceased:

Date of Birth: Date of Death:
Nature of passing:

Family visit: am/pm Day: Date:

Chief mourner:

Next of kin:

Address:

Postcode:

Email:

Phone:

Other family members/friends/chief executor:

Music

Wesley [ ]   Family Supplied [ ] Organ/piano [   ]

Obitus [ ]   Funeral Director [ ] Other [ ]

Processional

Title_____

Singer/Composer_____

Reflection

Title_____

Singer/Composer_____

Recessional

Title_____

Singer/Composer_____

Other Music

Hymns

Prayers or Blessings:

Readings/poems:

Tribute speakers:

Ritual/s:

Donations:

Funeral Tea:

Acknowledgements:

Ashes: Interment [   ] Scattering [   ]
Time:
Day and date:
Burial Site:

Funeral Director/Arranger:

[ ] Cremation

[ ] Burial

[ ] Memorial

Time:
Day:
Date of Ceremony:

Ceremony Venue:

Order of Service printed? Yes [ ] No [ ]
Due to Funeral Director by:

Curtain Open [ ]
Curtain Closed [ ]
Interment Music [ ]

Notes

Name of Deceased:

Date of Birth: Date of Death:
Nature of passing:

Family visit: am/pm Day: Date:

Chief mourner:

Next of kin:

Address:

Postcode:

Email:

Phone:

Other family members/friends/chief executor:

Music

Wesley [ ]   Family Supplied [ ] Organ/piano [ ]

Obitus [ ]   Funeral Director [ ]   Other [ ]

Processional

Title_____

Singer/Composer_____

Reflection

Title_____

Singer/Composer_____

Recessional

Title_____

Singer/Composer_____

Other Music

Hymns

Prayers or Blessings:

Readings/poems:

Tribute speakers:

Ritual/s:

Donations:

Funeral Tea:

Acknowledgements:

Ashes: Interment [   ]   Scattering [   ]
Time:
Day and date:
Burial Site:

Funeral Director/Arranger:

[ ] Cremation

[ ] Burial

[ ] Memorial

Time:
Day:
Date of Ceremony:

Ceremony Venue:

Order of Service printed? Yes [ ] No [ ]
Due to Funeral Director by:

Curtain Open [ ]
Curtain Closed [ ]
Interment Music [ ]

Notes

Name of Deceased:

Date of Birth: Date of Death:
Nature of passing:

Family visit: am/pm Day: Date:

Chief mourner:

Next of kin:

Address:

Postcode:

Email:

Phone:

Other family members/friends/chief executor:

Music

Wesley [ ]   Family Supplied [ ] Organ/piano [   ]

Obitus [ ]   Funeral Director [ ]   Other [ ]

Processional

Title_____

Singer/Composer_____

Reflection

Title_____

Singer/Composer_____

Recessional

Title_____

Singer/Composer_____

Other Music

Hymns

Prayers or Blessings:

Readings/poems:

Tribute speakers:

Ritual/s:

Donations:

Funeral Tea:

Acknowledgements:

Ashes: Interment [   ]   Scattering [   ]
Time:
Day and date:
Burial Site:

Funeral Director/Arranger:

[ ] Cremation

[ ] Burial

[ ] Memorial

Time:
Day:
Date of Ceremony:

Ceremony Venue:

Order of Service printed? Yes [ ] No [ ]
Due to Funeral Director by:

Curtain Open [ ]
Curtain Closed [ ]
Interment Music [ ]

Notes

Name of Deceased:

Date of Birth: Date of Death:
Nature of passing:

Family visit: am/pm Day: Date:

Chief mourner:

Next of kin:

Address:

Postcode:

Email:

Phone:

Other family members/friends/chief executor:

Music

Wesley [ ]   Family Supplied [ ] Organ/piano [ ]

Obitus [ ]   Funeral Director [ ] Other [ ]

Processional

Title_____

Singer/Composer_____

Reflection

Title_____

Singer/Composer_____

Recessional

Title_____

Singer/Composer_____

Other Music

Hymns

Prayers or Blessings:

Readings/poems:

Tribute speakers:

Ritual/s:

Donations:

Funeral Tea:

Acknowledgements:

Ashes: Interment [ ] Scattering [ ]
Time:
Day and date:
Burial Site:

Funeral Director/Arranger:

[ ] Cremation

[ ] Burial

[ ] Memorial

Time:
Day:
Date of Ceremony:

Ceremony Venue:

Order of Service printed? Yes [ ] No [ ]
Due to Funeral Director by:

Curtain Open [ ]
Curtain Closed [ ]
Interment Music [ ]

Notes

Name of Deceased:

Date of Birth: Date of Death:
Nature of passing:

Family visit: am/pm Day: Date:

Chief mourner:

Next of kin:

Address:

Postcode:

Email:

Phone:

Other family members/friends/chief executor:

Music

Wesley [ ]   Family Supplied [ ] Organ/piano [   ]

Obitus [ ]   Funeral Director [ ]   Other [ ]

Processional

Title_____

Singer/Composer_____

Reflection

Title_____

Singer/Composer_____

Recessional

Title_____

Singer/Composer_____

Other Music

Hymns

Prayers or Blessings:

Readings/poems:

Tribute speakers:

Ritual/s:

Donations:

Funeral Tea:

Acknowledgements:

Ashes: Interment [   ] Scattering [   ]
Time:
Day and date:
Burial Site:

Funeral Director/Arranger:

[ ] Cremation

[ ] Burial

[ ] Memorial

Time:
Day:
Date of Ceremony:

Ceremony Venue:

Order of Service printed? Yes [ ] No [ ]
Due to Funeral Director by:

Curtain Open [ ]
Curtain Closed [ ]
Interment Music [ ]

Notes

Name of Deceased:

Date of Birth: Date of Death:
Nature of passing:

Family visit: am/pm Day: Date:

Chief mourner:

Next of kin:

Address:

Postcode:

Email:

Phone:

Other family members/friends/chief executor:

Music

Wesley [ ]   Family Supplied [ ] Organ/piano [   ]

Obitus   [ ]   Funeral Director [ ]   Other [ ]

Processional

Title_____

Singer/Composer_____

Reflection

Title_____

Singer/Composer_____

Recessional

Title_____

Singer/Composer_____

Other Music

Hymns

Prayers or Blessings:

Readings/poems:

Tribute speakers:

Ritual/s:

Donations:

Funeral Tea:

Acknowledgements:

Ashes: Interment [   ]   Scattering [   ]
Time:
Day and date:
Burial Site:

Funeral Director/Arranger:

[ ] Cremation

[ ] Burial

[ ] Memorial

Time:
Day:
Date of Ceremony:

Ceremony Venue:

Order of Service printed? Yes [ ] No [ ]
Due to Funeral Director by:

Curtain Open [ ]
Curtain Closed [ ]
Interment Music [ ]

Notes

Name of Deceased:

Date of Birth: Date of Death:
Nature of passing:

Family visit: am/pm Day: Date:

Chief mourner:

Next of kin:

Address:

Postcode:

Email:

Phone:

Other family members/friends/chief executor:

Music

Wesley [ ]   Family Supplied [ ] Organ/piano [   ]

Obitus [ ]   Funeral Director [ ]   Other [ ]

Processional

Title_____

Singer/Composer_____

Reflection

Title_____

Singer/Composer_____

Recessional

Title_____

Singer/Composer_____

Other Music

Hymns

Prayers or Blessings:

Readings/poems:

Tribute speakers:

Ritual/s:

Donations:

Funeral Tea:

Acknowledgements:

Ashes: Interment [   ]   Scattering [   ]
Time:
Day and date:
Burial Site:

Funeral Director/Arranger:

[ ] Cremation

[ ] Burial

[ ] Memorial

Time:
Day:
Date of Ceremony:

Ceremony Venue:

Order of Service printed? Yes [ ] No [ ]
Due to Funeral Director by:

Curtain Open [ ]
Curtain Closed [ ]
Interment Music [ ]

Notes

Name of Deceased:

Date of Birth: Date of Death:
Nature of passing:

Family visit: am/pm Day: Date:

Chief mourner:

Next of kin:

Address:

Postcode:

Email:

Phone:

Other family members/friends/chief executor:

Music

Wesley [ ]   Family Supplied [ ] Organ/piano [ ]

Obitus [ ]   Funeral Director [ ]   Other [ ]

Processional

Title_____

Singer/Composer_____

Reflection

Title_____

Singer/Composer_____

Recessional

Title_____

Singer/Composer_____

Other Music

Hymns

Prayers or Blessings:

Readings/poems:

Tribute speakers:

Ritual/s:

Donations:

Funeral Tea:

Acknowledgements:

Ashes: Interment [ ] Scattering [ ]
Time:
Day and date:
Burial Site:

Funeral Director/Arranger:

[ ] Cremation

[ ] Burial

[ ] Memorial

Time:
Day:
Date of Ceremony:

Ceremony Venue:

Order of Service printed? Yes [ ] No [ ]
Due to Funeral Director by:

Curtain Open [ ]
Curtain Closed [ ]
Interment Music [ ]

Notes

Name of Deceased:

Date of Birth: Date of Death:
Nature of passing:

Family visit: am/pm Day: Date:

Chief mourner:

Next of kin:

Address:

Postcode:

Email:

Phone:

Other family members/friends/chief executor:

Music

Wesley [ ]   Family Supplied [ ] Organ/piano [   ]

Obitus   [ ]   Funeral Director [ ]   Other [ ]

Processional

Title_____

Singer/Composer_____

Reflection

Title_____

Singer/Composer_____

Recessional

Title_____

Singer/Composer_____

Other Music

Hymns

Prayers or Blessings:

Readings/poems:

Tribute speakers:

Ritual/s:

Donations:

Funeral Tea:

Acknowledgements:

Ashes: Interment [   ]   Scattering [   ]
Time:
Day and date:
Burial Site:

Funeral Director/Arranger:

[ ] Cremation

[ ] Burial

[ ] Memorial

Time:
Day:
Date of Ceremony:

Ceremony Venue:

Order of Service printed? Yes [ ] No [ ]
Due to Funeral Director by:

Curtain Open [ ]
Curtain Closed [ ]
Interment Music [ ]

Notes

Name of Deceased:

Date of Birth: Date of Death:
Nature of passing:

Family visit: am/pm Day: Date:

Chief mourner:

Next of kin:

Address:

Postcode:

Email:

Phone:

Other family members/friends/chief executor:

Music

Wesley [ ]   Family Supplied [ ] Organ/piano [   ]

Obitus [ ]   Funeral Director [ ]   Other [ ]

Processional

Title_____

Singer/Composer_____

Reflection

Title_____

Singer/Composer_____

Recessional

Title_____

Singer/Composer_____

Other Music

Hymns

Prayers or Blessings:

Readings/poems:

Tribute speakers:

Ritual/s:

Donations:

Funeral Tea:

Acknowledgements:

Ashes: Interment [   ]   Scattering [   ]
Time:
Day and date:
Burial Site:

Funeral Director/Arranger:

[ ] Cremation

[ ] Burial

[ ] Memorial

Time:
Day:
Date of Ceremony:

Ceremony Venue:

Order of Service printed? Yes [ ] No [ ]
Due to Funeral Director by:

Curtain Open [ ]
Curtain Closed [ ]
Interment Music [ ]

Notes

Name of Deceased:

Date of Birth: Date of Death:
Nature of passing:

Family visit: am/pm Day: Date:

Chief mourner:

Next of kin:

Address:

Postcode:

Email:

Phone:

Other family members/friends/chief executor:

Music

Wesley [ ]   Family Supplied [ ] Organ/piano [   ]

Obitus   [ ]   Funeral Director [ ]   Other [ ]

Processional

Title_____

Singer/Composer_____

Reflection

Title_____

Singer/Composer_____

Recessional

Title_____

Singer/Composer_____

Other Music

Hymns

Prayers or Blessings:

Readings/poems:

Tribute speakers:

Ritual/s:

Donations:

Funeral Tea:

Acknowledgements:

Ashes: Interment [   ] Scattering [   ]
Time:
Day and date:
Burial Site:

Funeral Director/Arranger:

[ ] Cremation

[ ] Burial

[ ] Memorial

Time:
Day:
Date of Ceremony:

Ceremony Venue:

Order of Service printed? Yes [ ] No [ ]
Due to Funeral Director by:

Curtain Open [ ]
Curtain Closed [ ]
Interment Music [ ]

Notes

Name of Deceased:

Date of Birth: Date of Death:
Nature of passing:

Family visit: am/pm Day: Date:

Chief mourner:

Next of kin:

Address:

Postcode:

Email:

Phone:

Other family members/friends/chief executor:

Music

Wesley [ ]   Family Supplied [ ] Organ/piano [ ]

Obitus [ ]   Funeral Director [ ] Other [ ]

Processional

Title_____

Singer/Composer_____

Reflection

Title_____

Singer/Composer_____

Recessional

Title_____

Singer/Composer_____

Other Music

Hymns

Prayers or Blessings:

Readings/poems:

Tribute speakers:

Ritual/s:

Donations:

Funeral Tea:

Acknowledgements:

Ashes: Interment [ ]   Scattering [ ]
Time:
Day and date:
Burial Site:

Funeral Director/Arranger:

[ ] Cremation

[ ] Burial

[ ] Memorial

Time:
Day:
Date of Ceremony:

Ceremony Venue:

Order of Service printed? Yes [ ] No [ ]
Due to Funeral Director by:

Curtain Open [ ]
Curtain Closed [ ]
Interment Music [ ]

Notes

Name of Deceased:

Date of Birth: Date of Death:
Nature of passing:

Family visit: am/pm Day: Date:

Chief mourner:

Next of kin:

Address:

Postcode:

Email:

Phone:

Other family members/friends/chief executor:

Music

Wesley [ ]   Family Supplied [ ] Organ/piano [ ]

Obitus [ ]   Funeral Director [ ] Other [ ]

Processional

Title_____

Singer/Composer_____

Reflection

Title_____

Singer/Composer_____

Recessional

Title_____

Singer/Composer_____

Other Music

Hymns

Prayers or Blessings:

Readings/poems:

Tribute speakers:

Ritual/s:

Donations:

Funeral Tea:

Acknowledgements:

Ashes: Interment [   ]   Scattering [   ]
Time:
Day and date:
Burial Site:

Funeral Director/Arranger:

[ ] Cremation

[ ] Burial

[ ] Memorial

Time:
Day:
Date of Ceremony:

Ceremony Venue:

Order of Service printed? Yes [ ] No [ ]
Due to Funeral Director by:

Curtain Open [ ]
Curtain Closed [ ]
Interment Music [ ]

Notes

Name of Deceased:

Date of Birth: Date of Death:
Nature of passing:

Family visit: am/pm Day: Date:

Chief mourner:

Next of kin:

Address:

Postcode:

Email:

Phone:

Other family members/friends/chief executor:

Music

Wesley [ ]   Family Supplied [ ] Organ/piano [   ]

Obitus   [ ]   Funeral Director [ ]   Other [ ]

Processional

Title_____

Singer/Composer_____

Reflection

Title_____

Singer/Composer_____

Recessional

Title_____

Singer/Composer_____

Other Music

Hymns

Prayers or Blessings:

Readings/poems:

Tribute speakers:

Ritual/s:

Donations:

Funeral Tea:

Acknowledgements:

Ashes: Interment [   ]   Scattering [   ]
Time:
Day and date:
Burial Site:

Funeral Director/Arranger:

[ ] Cremation

[ ] Burial

[ ] Memorial

Time:
Day:
Date of Ceremony:

Ceremony Venue:

Order of Service printed? Yes [ ] No [ ]
Due to Funeral Director by:

Curtain Open [ ]
Curtain Closed [ ]
Interment Music [ ]

Notes

Name of Deceased:

Date of Birth: Date of Death:
Nature of passing:

Family visit: am/pm Day: Date:

Chief mourner:

Next of kin:

Address:

Postcode:

Email:

Phone:

Other family members/friends/chief executor:

Music

Wesley [ ]   Family Supplied [ ] Organ/piano [ ]

Obitus   [ ]   Funeral Director [ ]   Other [ ]

Processional

Title_____

Singer/Composer_____

Reflection

Title_____

Singer/Composer_____

Recessional

Title_____

Singer/Composer_____

Other Music

Hymns

Prayers or Blessings:

Readings/poems:

Tribute speakers:

Ritual/s:

Donations:

Funeral Tea:

Acknowledgements:

Ashes: Interment [   ]   Scattering [ ]
Time:
Day and date:
Burial Site:

Funeral Director/Arranger:

[ ] Cremation

[ ] Burial

[ ] Memorial

Time:
Day:
Date of Ceremony:

Ceremony Venue:

Order of Service printed? Yes [ ] No [ ]
Due to Funeral Director by:

Curtain Open [ ]
Curtain Closed [ ]
Interment Music [ ]

Notes

Name of Deceased:

Date of Birth: Date of Death:
Nature of passing:

Family visit: am/pm Day: Date:

Chief mourner:

Next of kin:

Address:

Postcode:

Email:

Phone:

Other family members/friends/chief executor:

Music

Wesley [ ]   Family Supplied [ ] Organ/piano [   ]

Obitus [ ]   Funeral Director [ ]   Other [ ]

Processional

Title_____

Singer/Composer_____

Reflection

Title_____

Singer/Composer_____

Recessional

Title_____

Singer/Composer_____

Other Music

Hymns

Prayers or Blessings:

Readings/poems:

Tribute speakers:

Ritual/s:

Donations:

Funeral Tea:

Acknowledgements:

Ashes: Interment [   ] Scattering [   ]
Time:
Day and date:
Burial Site:

Funeral Director/Arranger:

[ ] Cremation

[ ] Burial

[ ] Memorial

Time:
Day:
Date of Ceremony:

Ceremony Venue:

Order of Service printed? Yes [ ] No [ ]
Due to Funeral Director by:

Curtain Open [ ]
Curtain Closed [ ]
Interment Music [ ]

Notes

Name of Deceased:

Date of Birth: Date of Death:
Nature of passing:

Family visit: am/pm Day: Date:

Chief mourner:

Next of kin:

Address:

Postcode:

Email:

Phone:

Other family members/friends/chief executor:

Music

Wesley [ ] Family Supplied [ ] Organ/piano [ ]

Obitus [ ] Funeral Director [ ] Other [ ]

Processional

Title_____

Singer/Composer_____

Reflection

Title_____

Singer/Composer_____

Recessional

Title_____

Singer/Composer_____

Other Music

Hymns

Prayers or Blessings:

Readings/poems:

Tribute speakers:

Ritual/s:

Donations:

Funeral Tea:

Acknowledgements:

Ashes: Interment [ ] Scattering [ ]
Time:
Day and date:
Burial Site:

Funeral Director/Arranger:

[ ] Cremation

[ ] Burial

[ ] Memorial

Time:
Day:
Date of Ceremony:

Ceremony Venue:

Order of Service printed? Yes [ ] No [ ]
Due to Funeral Director by:

Curtain Open [ ]
Curtain Closed [ ]
Interment Music [ ]

Notes

Name of Deceased:

Date of Birth: Date of Death:
Nature of passing:

Family visit: am/pm Day: Date:

Chief mourner:

Next of kin:

Address:

Postcode:

Email:

Phone:

Other family members/friends/chief executor:

Music

Wesley [ ]   Family Supplied [ ] Organ/piano [   ]

Obitus [ ]   Funeral Director [ ] Other [ ]

Processional

Title_____

Singer/Composer_____

Reflection

Title_____

Singer/Composer_____

Recessional

Title_____

Singer/Composer_____

Other Music

Hymns

Prayers or Blessings:

Readings/poems:

Tribute speakers:

Ritual/s:

Donations:

Funeral Tea:

Acknowledgements:

Ashes: Interment [   ] Scattering [   ]
Time:
Day and date:
Burial Site:

Funeral Director/Arranger:

[ ] Cremation

[ ] Burial

[ ] Memorial

Time:
Day:
Date of Ceremony:

Ceremony Venue:

Order of Service printed? Yes [ ] No [ ]
Due to Funeral Director by:

Curtain Open [ ]
Curtain Closed [ ]
Interment Music [ ]

Notes

Name of Deceased:

Date of Birth: Date of Death:
Nature of passing:

Family visit: am/pm Day: Date:

Chief mourner:

Next of kin:

Address:

Postcode:

Email:

Phone:

Other family members/friends/chief executor:

Music

Wesley [ ]   Family Supplied [ ] Organ/piano [   ]

Obitus [ ]   Funeral Director [ ] Other [ ]

Processional

Title_____

Singer/Composer_____

Reflection

Title_____

Singer/Composer_____

Recessional

Title_____

Singer/Composer_____

Other Music

Hymns

Prayers or Blessings:

Readings/poems:

Tribute speakers:

Ritual/s:

Donations:

Funeral Tea:

Acknowledgements:

Ashes: Interment [   ] Scattering [   ]
Time:
Day and date:
Burial Site:

Funeral Director/Arranger:

[ ] Cremation

[ ] Burial

[ ] Memorial

Time:
Day:
Date of Ceremony:

Ceremony Venue:

Order of Service printed? Yes [ ] No [ ]
Due to Funeral Director by:

Curtain Open [ ]
Curtain Closed [ ]
Interment Music [ ]

Notes

Name of Deceased:

Date of Birth: Date of Death:
Nature of passing:

Family visit: am/pm Day: Date:

Chief mourner:

Next of kin:

Address:

Postcode:

Email:

Phone:

Other family members/friends/chief executor:

Music

Wesley [ ]   Family Supplied [ ] Organ/piano [ ]

Obitus [ ]   Funeral Director [ ] Other [ ]

Processional

Title_____

Singer/Composer_____

Reflection

Title_____

Singer/Composer_____

Recessional

Title_____

Singer/Composer_____

Other Music

Hymns

Prayers or Blessings:

Readings/poems:

Tribute speakers:

Ritual/s:

Donations:

Funeral Tea:

Acknowledgements:

Ashes: Interment [   ]   Scattering [   ]
Time:
Day and date:
Burial Site:

Funeral Director/Arranger:

[ ] Cremation

[ ] Burial

[ ] Memorial

Time:
Day:
Date of Ceremony:

Ceremony Venue:

Order of Service printed? Yes [ ] No [ ]
Due to Funeral Director by:

Curtain Open [ ]
Curtain Closed [ ]
Interment Music [ ]

Notes

Name of Deceased:

Date of Birth: Date of Death:
Nature of passing:

Family visit: am/pm Day: Date:

Chief mourner:

Next of kin:

Address:

Postcode:

Email:

Phone:

Other family members/friends/chief executor:

Music

Wesley [ ]   Family Supplied [ ] Organ/piano [ ]

Obitus [ ]   Funeral Director [ ] Other [ ]

Processional

Title_____

Singer/Composer_____

Reflection

Title_____

Singer/Composer_____

Recessional

Title_____

Singer/Composer_____

Other Music

Hymns

Prayers or Blessings:

Readings/poems:

Tribute speakers:

Ritual/s:

Donations:

Funeral Tea:

Acknowledgements:

Ashes: Interment [   ] Scattering [   ]
Time:
Day and date:
Burial Site:

Funeral Director/Arranger:

[ ] Cremation

[ ] Burial

[ ] Memorial

Time:
Day:
Date of Ceremony:

Ceremony Venue:

Order of Service printed? Yes [ ] No [ ]
Due to Funeral Director by:

Curtain Open [ ]
Curtain Closed [ ]
Interment Music [ ]

Notes

Name of Deceased:

Date of Birth: Date of Death:
Nature of passing:

Family visit: am/pm Day: Date:

Chief mourner:

Next of kin:

Address:

Postcode:

Email:

Phone:

Other family members/friends/chief executor:

Music

Wesley [ ]   Family Supplied [ ] Organ/piano [   ]

Obitus [ ]   Funeral Director [ ] Other [ ]

Processional

Title_____

Singer/Composer_____

Reflection

Title_____

Singer/Composer_____

Recessional

Title_____

Singer/Composer_____

Other Music

Hymns

Prayers or Blessings:

Readings/poems:

Tribute speakers:

Ritual/s:

Donations:

Funeral Tea:

Acknowledgements:

Ashes: Interment [   ]   Scattering [   ]
Time:
Day and date:
Burial Site:

Funeral Director/Arranger:

[ ] Cremation

[ ] Burial

[ ] Memorial

Time:
Day:
Date of Ceremony:

Ceremony Venue:

Order of Service printed? Yes [ ] No [ ]
Due to Funeral Director by:

Curtain Open [ ]
Curtain Closed [ ]
Interment Music [ ]

Notes

Name of Deceased:

Date of Birth: Date of Death:
Nature of passing:

Family visit: am/pm Day: Date:

Chief mourner:

Next of kin:

Address:

Postcode:

Email:

Phone:

Other family members/friends/chief executor:

Music

Wesley [ ]   Family Supplied [ ] Organ/piano [   ]

Obitus [ ]   Funeral Director [ ] Other [ ]

Processional

Title_____

Singer/Composer_____

Reflection

Title_____

Singer/Composer_____

Recessional

Title_____

Singer/Composer_____

Other Music

Hymns

Prayers or Blessings:

Readings/poems:

Tribute speakers:

Ritual/s:

Donations:

Funeral Tea:

Acknowledgements:

Ashes: Interment [   ]   Scattering [   ]
Time:
Day and date:
Burial Site:

Funeral Director/Arranger:

[ ] Cremation

[ ] Burial

[ ] Memorial

Time:
Day:
Date of Ceremony:

Ceremony Venue:

Order of Service printed? Yes [ ] No [ ]
Due to Funeral Director by:

Curtain Open [ ]
Curtain Closed [ ]
Interment Music [ ]

Notes

Name of Deceased:

Date of Birth: Date of Death:
Nature of passing:

Family visit: am/pm Day: Date:

Chief mourner:

Next of kin:

Address:

Postcode:

Email:

Phone:

Other family members/friends/chief executor:

Music

Wesley [ ]   Family Supplied [ ] Organ/piano [   ]

Obitus   [ ]   Funeral Director [ ] Other [ ]

Processional

Title_____

Singer/Composer_____

Reflection

Title_____

Singer/Composer_____

Recessional

Title_____

Singer/Composer_____

Other Music

Hymns

Prayers or Blessings:

Readings/poems:

Tribute speakers:

Ritual/s:

Donations:

Funeral Tea:

Acknowledgements:

Ashes: Interment [   ] Scattering [ ]
Time:
Day and date:
Burial Site:

Funeral Director/Arranger:

[ ] Cremation

[ ] Burial

[ ] Memorial

Time:
Day:
Date of Ceremony:

Ceremony Venue:

Order of Service printed? Yes [ ] No [ ]
Due to Funeral Director by:

Curtain Open [ ]
Curtain Closed [ ]
Interment Music [ ]

Notes

Name of Deceased:

Date of Birth: Date of Death:
Nature of passing:

Family visit: am/pm Day: Date:

Chief mourner:

Next of kin:

Address:

Postcode:

Email:

Phone:

Other family members/friends/chief executor:

Music

Wesley [ ]   Family Supplied [ ] Organ/piano [   ]

Obitus   [ ]   Funeral Director [ ]   Other [ ]

Processional

Title_____

Singer/Composer_____

Reflection

Title_____

Singer/Composer_____

Recessional

Title_____

Singer/Composer_____

Other Music

Hymns

Prayers or Blessings:

Readings/poems:

Tribute speakers:

Ritual/s:

Donations:

Funeral Tea:

Acknowledgements:

Ashes: Interment [   ]   Scattering [   ]
Time:
Day and date:
Burial Site:

Funeral Director/Arranger:

[ ] Cremation

[ ] Burial

[ ] Memorial

Time:
Day:
Date of Ceremony:

Ceremony Venue:

Order of Service printed? Yes [ ] No [ ]
Due to Funeral Director by:

Curtain Open [ ]
Curtain Closed [ ]
Interment Music [ ]

Notes

Name of Deceased:

Date of Birth: Date of Death:
Nature of passing:

Family visit: am/pm Day: Date:

Chief mourner:

Next of kin:

Address:

Postcode:

Email:

Phone:

Other family members/friends/chief executor:

130

Music

Wesley [ ]   Family Supplied [ ] Organ/piano [   ]

Obitus   [ ]   Funeral Director [ ]   Other [ ]

Processional

Title_____

Singer/Composer_____

Reflection

Title_____

Singer/Composer_____

Recessional

Title_____

Singer/Composer_____

Other Music

Hymns

Prayers or Blessings:

Readings/poems:

Tribute speakers:

Ritual/s:

Donations:

Funeral Tea:

Acknowledgements:

Ashes: Interment [   ]   Scattering [   ]
Time:
Day and date:
Burial Site:

Funeral Director/Arranger:

[ ] Cremation

[ ] Burial

[ ] Memorial

Time:
Day:
Date of Ceremony:

Ceremony Venue:

Order of Service printed? Yes [ ] No [ ]
Due to Funeral Director by:

Curtain Open [ ]
Curtain Closed [ ]
Interment Music [ ]

Notes

Name of Deceased:

Date of Birth: Date of Death:
Nature of passing:

Family visit: am/pm Day: Date:

Chief mourner:

Next of kin:

Address:

Postcode:

Email:

Phone:

Other family members/friends/chief executor:

Music

Wesley [ ]   Family Supplied [ ] Organ/piano [   ]

Obitus [ ]   Funeral Director [ ] Other [ ]

Processional

Title_____

Singer/Composer_____

Reflection

Title_____

Singer/Composer_____

Recessional

Title_____

Singer/Composer_____

Other Music

Hymns

Prayers or Blessings:

Readings/poems:

Tribute speakers:

Ritual/s:

Donations:

Funeral Tea:

Acknowledgements:

Ashes: Interment [   ] Scattering [   ]
Time:
Day and date:
Burial Site:

Funeral Director/Arranger:

[ ] Cremation

[ ] Burial

[ ] Memorial

Time:
Day:
Date of Ceremony:

Ceremony Venue:

Order of Service printed? Yes [ ] No [ ]
Due to Funeral Director by:

Curtain Open [ ]
Curtain Closed [ ]
Interment Music [ ]

Notes

Name of Deceased:

Date of Birth: Date of Death:
Nature of passing:

Family visit: am/pm Day: Date:

Chief mourner:

Next of kin:

Address:

Postcode:

Email:

Phone:

Other family members/friends/chief executor:

Music

Wesley [ ]   Family Supplied [ ] Organ/piano [   ]

Obitus [ ]   Funeral Director [ ]   Other [ ]

Processional

Title_____

Singer/Composer_____

Reflection

Title_____

Singer/Composer_____

Recessional

Title_____

Singer/Composer_____

Other Music

Hymns

Prayers or Blessings:

Readings/poems:

Tribute speakers:

Ritual/s:

Donations:

Funeral Tea:

Acknowledgements:

Ashes: Interment [   ]   Scattering [   ]
Time:
Day and date:
Burial Site:

Funeral Director/Arranger:

[ ] Cremation

[ ] Burial

[ ] Memorial

Time:
Day:
Date of Ceremony:

Ceremony Venue:

Order of Service printed? Yes [ ] No [ ]
Due to Funeral Director by:

Curtain Open [ ]
Curtain Closed [ ]
Interment Music [ ]

Notes

Name of Deceased:

Date of Birth: Date of Death:
Nature of passing:

Family visit: am/pm Day: Date:

Chief mourner:

Next of kin:

Address:

Postcode:

Email:

Phone:

Other family members/friends/chief executor:

Music

Wesley [ ]   Family Supplied [ ] Organ/piano [   ]

Obitus   [ ]   Funeral Director [ ]   Other [ ]

Processional

Title_____

Singer/Composer_____

Reflection

Title_____

Singer/Composer_____

Recessional

Title_____

Singer/Composer_____

Other Music

Hymns

Prayers or Blessings:

Readings/poems:

Tribute speakers:

Ritual/s:

Donations:

Funeral Tea:

Acknowledgements:

Ashes: Interment [   ]   Scattering [   ]
Time:
Day and date:
Burial Site:

Funeral Director/Arranger:

[ ] Cremation

[ ] Burial

[ ] Memorial

Time:
Day:
Date of Ceremony:

Ceremony Venue:

Order of Service printed? Yes [ ] No [ ]
Due to Funeral Director by:

Curtain Open [ ]
Curtain Closed [ ]
Interment Music [ ]

Notes

Name of Deceased:

Date of Birth: Date of Death:
Nature of passing:

Family visit: am/pm Day: Date:

Chief mourner:

Next of kin:

Address:

Postcode:

Email:

Phone:

Other family members/friends/chief executor:

Music

Wesley [ ]   Family Supplied [ ] Organ/piano [   ]

Obitus [ ]   Funeral Director [ ]   Other [ ]

Processional

Title_____

Singer/Composer_____

Reflection

Title_____

Singer/Composer_____

Recessional

Title_____

Singer/Composer_____

Other Music

Hymns

Prayers or Blessings:

Readings/poems:

Tribute speakers:

Ritual/s:

Donations:

Funeral Tea:

Acknowledgements:

Ashes: Interment [   ]   Scattering [   ]
Time:
Day and date:
Burial Site:

Funeral Director/Arranger:

[ ] Cremation

[ ] Burial

[ ] Memorial

Time:
Day:
Date of Ceremony:

Ceremony Venue:

Order of Service printed? Yes [ ] No [ ]
Due to Funeral Director by:

Curtain Open [ ]
Curtain Closed [ ]
Interment Music [ ]

Notes

Name of Deceased:

Date of Birth: Date of Death:
Nature of passing:

Family visit: am/pm Day: Date:

Chief mourner:

Next of kin:

Address:

Postcode:

Email:

Phone:

Other family members/friends/chief executor:

Music

Wesley [ ]   Family Supplied [ ] Organ/piano [ ]

Obitus [ ]   Funeral Director [ ] Other [ ]

Processional

Title_____

Singer/Composer_____

Reflection

Title_____

Singer/Composer_____

Recessional

Title_____

Singer/Composer_____

Other Music

Hymns

Prayers or Blessings:

Readings/poems:

Tribute speakers:

Ritual/s:

Donations:

Funeral Tea:

Acknowledgements:

Ashes: Interment [ ] Scattering [ ]
Time:
Day and date:
Burial Site:

Funeral Director/Arranger:

[ ] Cremation

[ ] Burial

[ ] Memorial

Time:
Day:
Date of Ceremony:

Ceremony Venue:

Order of Service printed? Yes [ ] No [ ]
Due to Funeral Director by:

Curtain Open [ ]
Curtain Closed [ ]
Interment Music [ ]

Notes

Name of Deceased:

Date of Birth: Date of Death:
Nature of passing:

Family visit: am/pm Day: Date:

Chief mourner:

Next of kin:

Address:

Postcode:

Email:

Phone:

Other family members/friends/chief executor:

Music

Wesley [ ]   Family Supplied [ ] Organ/piano [   ]

Obitus [ ]   Funeral Director [ ]   Other [ ]

Processional

Title_____

Singer/Composer_____

Reflection

Title_____

Singer/Composer_____

Recessional

Title_____

Singer/Composer_____

Other Music

Hymns

Prayers or Blessings:

Readings/poems:

Tribute speakers:

Ritual/s:

Donations:

Funeral Tea:

Acknowledgements:

Ashes: Interment [   ]   Scattering [   ]
Time:
Day and date:
Burial Site:

Funeral Director/Arranger:

[ ] Cremation

[ ] Burial

[ ] Memorial

Time:
Day:
Date of Ceremony:

Ceremony Venue:

Order of Service printed? Yes [ ] No [ ]
Due to Funeral Director by:

Curtain Open [ ]
Curtain Closed [ ]
Interment Music [ ]

Notes

Name of Deceased:

Date of Birth: Date of Death:
Nature of passing:

Family visit: am/pm Day: Date:

Chief mourner:

Next of kin:

Address:

Postcode:

Email:

Phone:

Other family members/friends/chief executor:

Music

Wesley [ ]   Family Supplied [ ] Organ/piano [   ]

Obitus   [ ]   Funeral Director [ ] Other [ ]

Processional

Title_____

Singer/Composer_____

Reflection

Title_____

Singer/Composer_____

Recessional

Title_____

Singer/Composer_____

Other Music

Hymns

Prayers or Blessings:

Readings/poems:

Tribute speakers:

Ritual/s:

Donations:

Funeral Tea:

Acknowledgements:

Ashes: Interment [   ] Scattering [   ]
Time:
Day and date:
Burial Site:

Funeral Director/Arranger:

[ ] Cremation

[ ] Burial

[ ] Memorial

Time:
Day:
Date of Ceremony:

Ceremony Venue:

Order of Service printed? Yes [ ] No [ ]
Due to Funeral Director by:

Curtain Open [ ]
Curtain Closed [ ]
Interment Music [ ]

Notes

Name of Deceased:

Date of Birth: Date of Death:
Nature of passing:

Family visit: am/pm Day: Date:

Chief mourner:

Next of kin:

Address:

Postcode:

Email:

Phone:

Other family members/friends/chief executor:

Music

Wesley [ ]   Family Supplied [ ] Organ/piano [ ]

Obitus   [ ]   Funeral Director [ ]   Other [ ]

Processional

Title_____

Singer/Composer_____

Reflection

Title_____

Singer/Composer_____

Recessional

Title_____

Singer/Composer_____

Other Music

Hymns

Prayers or Blessings:

Readings/poems:

Tribute speakers:

Ritual/s:

Donations:

Funeral Tea:

Acknowledgements:

Ashes: Interment [   ]   Scattering [   ]
Time:
Day and date:
Burial Site:

Funeral Director/Arranger:

[ ] Cremation

[ ] Burial

[ ] Memorial

Time:
Day:
Date of Ceremony:

Ceremony Venue:

Order of Service printed? Yes [ ] No [ ]
Due to Funeral Director by:

Curtain Open [ ]
Curtain Closed [ ]
Interment Music [ ]

Notes

Name of Deceased:

Date of Birth: Date of Death:
Nature of passing:

Family visit: am/pm Day: Date:

Chief mourner:

Next of kin:

Address:

Postcode:

Email:

Phone:

Other family members/friends/chief executor:

Music

Wesley [ ]   Family Supplied [ ] Organ/piano [   ]

Obitus [ ]   Funeral Director [ ]   Other [ ]

Processional

Title_____

Singer/Composer_____

Reflection

Title_____

Singer/Composer_____

Recessional

Title_____

Singer/Composer_____

Other Music

Hymns

Prayers or Blessings:

Readings/poems:

Tribute speakers:

Ritual/s:

Donations:

Funeral Tea:

Acknowledgements:

Ashes: Interment [   ]   Scattering [   ]
Time:
Day and date:
Burial Site:

Funeral Director/Arranger:

[ ] Cremation

[ ] Burial

[ ] Memorial

Time:
Day:
Date of Ceremony:

Ceremony Venue:

Order of Service printed? Yes [ ] No [ ]
Due to Funeral Director by:

Curtain Open [ ]
Curtain Closed [ ]
Interment Music [ ]

Notes

Name of Deceased:

Date of Birth: Date of Death:
Nature of passing:

Family visit: am/pm Day: Date:

Chief mourner:

Next of kin:

Address:

Postcode:

Email:

Phone:

Other family members/friends/chief executor:

Music

Wesley [ ]   Family Supplied [ ] Organ/piano [   ]

Obitus   [ ]   Funeral Director [ ]   Other [ ]

Processional

Title_____

Singer/Composer_____

Reflection

Title_____

Singer/Composer_____

Recessional

Title_____

Singer/Composer_____

Other Music

Hymns

Prayers or Blessings:

Readings/poems:

Tribute speakers:

Ritual/s:

Donations:

Funeral Tea:

Acknowledgements:

Ashes: Interment [   ] Scattering [   ]
Time:
Day and date:
Burial Site:

Funeral Director/Arranger:

[ ] Cremation

[ ] Burial

[ ] Memorial

Time:
Day:
Date of Ceremony:

Ceremony Venue:

Order of Service printed? Yes [ ] No [ ]
Due to Funeral Director by:

Curtain Open [ ]
Curtain Closed [ ]
Interment Music [ ]

Notes

Name of Deceased:

Date of Birth: Date of Death:
Nature of passing:

Family visit: am/pm Day: Date:

Chief mourner:

Next of kin:

Address:

Postcode:

Email:

Phone:

Other family members/friends/chief executor:

Music

Wesley [ ]   Family Supplied [ ] Organ/piano [ ]

Obitus [ ]   Funeral Director [ ] Other [ ]

Processional

Title_____

Singer/Composer_____

Reflection

Title_____

Singer/Composer_____

Recessional

Title_____

Singer/Composer_____

Other Music

Hymns

Prayers or Blessings:

Readings/poems:

Tribute speakers:

Ritual/s:

Donations:

Funeral Tea:

Acknowledgements:

Ashes: Interment [   ]   Scattering [   ]
Time:
Day and date:
Burial Site:

Funeral Director/Arranger:

[ ] Cremation

[ ] Burial

[ ] Memorial

Time:
Day:
Date of Ceremony:

Ceremony Venue:

Order of Service printed? Yes [ ] No [ ]
Due to Funeral Director by:

Curtain Open [ ]
Curtain Closed [ ]
Interment Music [ ]

Notes

Name of Deceased:

Date of Birth: Date of Death:
Nature of passing:

Family visit: am/pm Day: Date:

Chief mourner:

Next of kin:

Address:

Postcode:

Email:

Phone:

Other family members/friends/chief executor:

Music

Wesley [ ]   Family Supplied [ ] Organ/piano [ ]

Obitus [ ]   Funeral Director [ ] Other [ ]

Processional

Title_____

Singer/Composer_____

Reflection

Title_____

Singer/Composer_____

Recessional

Title_____

Singer/Composer_____

Other Music

Hymns

Prayers or Blessings:

Readings/poems:

Tribute speakers:

Ritual/s:

Donations:

Funeral Tea:

Acknowledgements:

Ashes: Interment [ ] Scattering [ ]
Time:
Day and date:
Burial Site:

Funeral Director/Arranger:

[ ] Cremation

[ ] Burial

[ ] Memorial

Time:
Day:
Date of Ceremony:

Ceremony Venue:

Order of Service printed? Yes [ ] No [ ]
Due to Funeral Director by:

Curtain Open [ ]
Curtain Closed [ ]
Interment Music [ ]

Notes

Name of Deceased:

Date of Birth: Date of Death:
Nature of passing:

Family visit: am/pm Day: Date:

Chief mourner:

Next of kin:

Address:

Postcode:

Email:

Phone:

Other family members/friends/chief executor:

Music

Wesley [ ]   Family Supplied [ ] Organ/piano [ ]

Obitus [ ]   Funeral Director [ ] Other [ ]

Processional

Title_____

Singer/Composer_____

Reflection

Title_____

Singer/Composer_____

Recessional

Title_____

Singer/Composer_____

Other Music

Hymns

Prayers or Blessings:

Readings/poems:

Tribute speakers:

Ritual/s:

Donations:

Funeral Tea:

Acknowledgements:

Ashes: Interment [   ]   Scattering [   ]
Time:
Day and date:
Burial Site:

Funeral Director/Arranger:

[ ] Cremation

[ ] Burial

[ ] Memorial

Time:
Day:
Date of Ceremony:

Ceremony Venue:

Order of Service printed? Yes [ ] No [ ]
Due to Funeral Director by:

Curtain Open [ ]
Curtain Closed [ ]
Interment Music [ ]

Notes

Name of Deceased:

Date of Birth: Date of Death:
Nature of passing:

Family visit: am/pm Day: Date:

Chief mourner:

Next of kin:

Address:

Postcode:

Email:

Phone:

Other family members/friends/chief executor:

Music

Wesley [ ] Family Supplied [ ] Organ/piano [ ]

Obitus [ ] Funeral Director [ ] Other [ ]

Processional

Title_____

Singer/Composer_____

Reflection

Title_____

Singer/Composer_____

Recessional

Title_____

Singer/Composer_____

Other Music

Hymns

Prayers or Blessings:

Readings/poems:

Tribute speakers:

Ritual/s:

Donations:

Funeral Tea:

Acknowledgements:

Ashes: Interment [ ] Scattering [ ]
Time:
Day and date:
Burial Site:

Funeral Director/Arranger:

[ ] Cremation

[ ] Burial

[ ] Memorial

Time:
Day:
Date of Ceremony:

Ceremony Venue:

Order of Service printed? Yes [ ] No [ ]
Due to Funeral Director by:

Curtain Open [ ]
Curtain Closed [ ]
Interment Music [ ]

Notes

Name of Deceased:

Date of Birth: Date of Death:
Nature of passing:

Family visit: am/pm Day: Date:

Chief mourner:

Next of kin:

Address:

Postcode:

Email:

Phone:

Other family members/friends/chief executor:

Music

Wesley [ ]   Family Supplied [ ] Organ/piano [   ]

Obitus [ ]   Funeral Director [ ] Other [ ]

Processional

Title_____

Singer/Composer_____

Reflection

Title_____

Singer/Composer_____

Recessional

Title_____

Singer/Composer_____

Other Music

Hymns

Prayers or Blessings:

Readings/poems:

Tribute speakers:

Ritual/s:

Donations:

Funeral Tea:

Acknowledgements:

Ashes: Interment [   ] Scattering [   ]
Time:
Day and date:
Burial Site:

Funeral Director/Arranger:

[ ] Cremation

[ ] Burial

[ ] Memorial

Time:
Day:
Date of Ceremony:

Ceremony Venue:

Order of Service printed? Yes [ ] No [ ]
Due to Funeral Director by:

Curtain Open [ ]
Curtain Closed [ ]
Interment Music [ ]

Notes

Name of Deceased:

Date of Birth: Date of Death:
Nature of passing:

Family visit: am/pm Day: Date:

Chief mourner:

Next of kin:

Address:

Postcode:

Email:

Phone:

Other family members/friends/chief executor:

Music

Wesley [ ]   Family Supplied [ ] Organ/piano [   ]

Obitus [ ]   Funeral Director [ ]   Other [ ]

Processional

Title_____

Singer/Composer_____

Reflection

Title_____

Singer/Composer_____

Recessional

Title_____

Singer/Composer_____

Other Music

Hymns

Prayers or Blessings:

Readings/poems:

Tribute speakers:

Ritual/s:

Donations:

Funeral Tea:

Acknowledgements:

Ashes: Interment [   ] Scattering [   ]
Time:
Day and date:
Burial Site:

Funeral Director/Arranger:

[ ] Cremation

[ ] Burial

[ ] Memorial

Time:
Day:
Date of Ceremony:

Ceremony Venue:

Order of Service printed? Yes [ ] No [ ]
Due to Funeral Director by:

Curtain Open [ ]
Curtain Closed [ ]
Interment Music [ ]

Notes

Name of Deceased:

Date of Birth: Date of Death:
Nature of passing:

Family visit: am/pm Day: Date:

Chief mourner:

Next of kin:

Address:

Postcode:

Email:

Phone:

Other family members/friends/chief executor:

Music

Wesley [ ]   Family Supplied [ ] Organ/piano [   ]

Obitus [ ]   Funeral Director [ ] Other [ ]

Processional

Title_____

Singer/Composer_____

Reflection

Title_____

Singer/Composer_____

Recessional

Title_____

Singer/Composer_____

Other Music

Hymns

Prayers or Blessings:

Readings/poems:

Tribute speakers:

Ritual/s:

Donations:

Funeral Tea:

Acknowledgements:

Ashes: Interment [   ] Scattering [   ]
Time:
Day and date:
Burial Site:

Funeral Director/Arranger:

[ ] Cremation

[ ] Burial

[ ] Memorial

Time:
Day:
Date of Ceremony:

Ceremony Venue:

Order of Service printed? Yes [ ] No [ ]
Due to Funeral Director by:

Curtain Open [ ]
Curtain Closed [ ]
Interment Music [ ]

Notes

Name of Deceased:

Date of Birth: Date of Death:
Nature of passing:

Family visit: am/pm Day: Date:

Chief mourner:

Next of kin:

Address:

Postcode:

Email:

Phone:

Other family members/friends/chief executor:

Music

Wesley [ ]   Family Supplied [ ] Organ/piano [   ]

Obitus [ ]   Funeral Director [ ]   Other [ ]

Processional

Title_____

Singer/Composer_____

Reflection

Title_____

Singer/Composer_____

Recessional

Title_____

Singer/Composer_____

Other Music

Hymns

Prayers or Blessings:

Readings/poems:

Tribute speakers:

Ritual/s:

Donations:

Funeral Tea:

Acknowledgements:

Ashes: Interment [   ]   Scattering [   ]
Time:
Day and date:
Burial Site:

Funeral Director/Arranger:

[ ] Cremation

[ ] Burial

[ ] Memorial

Time:
Day:
Date of Ceremony:

Ceremony Venue:

Order of Service printed? Yes [ ] No [ ]
Due to Funeral Director by:

Curtain Open [ ]
Curtain Closed [ ]
Interment Music [ ]

Notes

Name of Deceased:

Date of Birth: Date of Death:
Nature of passing:

Family visit: am/pm Day: Date:

Chief mourner:

Next of kin:

Address:

Postcode:

Email:

Phone:

Other family members/friends/chief executor:

Music

Wesley [ ]   Family Supplied [ ] Organ/piano [ ]

Obitus [ ]   Funeral Director [ ] Other [ ]

Processional

Title_____

Singer/Composer_____

Reflection

Title_____

Singer/Composer_____

Recessional

Title_____

Singer/Composer_____

Other Music

Hymns

Prayers or Blessings:

Readings/poems:

Tribute speakers:

Ritual/s:

Donations:

Funeral Tea:

Acknowledgements:

Ashes: Interment [　]　Scattering [　]
Time:
Day and date:
Burial Site:

Funeral Director/Arranger:

[ ] Cremation

[ ] Burial

[ ] Memorial

Time:
Day:
Date of Ceremony:

Ceremony Venue:

Order of Service printed? Yes [ ] No [ ]
Due to Funeral Director by:

Curtain Open [ ]
Curtain Closed [ ]
Interment Music [ ]

Notes

Name of Deceased:

Date of Birth: Date of Death:
Nature of passing:

Family visit: am/pm Day: Date:

Chief mourner:

Next of kin:

Address:

Postcode:

Email:

Phone:

Other family members/friends/chief executor:

Music

Wesley [ ]   Family Supplied [ ] Organ/piano [ ]

Obitus [ ]   Funeral Director [ ]   Other [ ]

Processional

Title_____

Singer/Composer_____

Reflection

Title_____

Singer/Composer_____

Recessional

Title_____

Singer/Composer_____

Other Music

Hymns

Prayers or Blessings:

Readings/poems:

Tribute speakers:

Ritual/s:

Donations:

Funeral Tea:

Acknowledgements:

Ashes: Interment [ ]   Scattering [ ]
Time:
Day and date:
Burial Site:

Funeral Director/Arranger:

[ ] Cremation

[ ] Burial

[ ] Memorial

Time:
Day:
Date of Ceremony:

Ceremony Venue:

Order of Service printed? Yes [ ] No [ ]
Due to Funeral Director by:

Curtain Open [ ]
Curtain Closed [ ]
Interment Music [ ]

Notes

Name of Deceased:

Date of Birth: Date of Death:
Nature of passing:

Family visit: am/pm Day: Date:

Chief mourner:

Next of kin:

Address:

Postcode:

Email:

Phone:

Other family members/friends/chief executor:

Music

Wesley [ ] Family Supplied [ ] Organ/piano [ ]

Obitus [ ] Funeral Director [ ] Other [ ]

Processional

Title_____

Singer/Composer_____

Reflection

Title_____

Singer/Composer_____

Recessional

Title_____

Singer/Composer_____

Other Music

Hymns

Prayers or Blessings:

Readings/poems:

Tribute speakers:

Ritual/s:

Donations:

Funeral Tea:

Acknowledgements:

Ashes: Interment [   ] Scattering [   ]
Time:
Day and date:
Burial Site:

Funeral Director/Arranger:

[ ] Cremation

[ ] Burial

[ ] Memorial

Time:
Day:
Date of Ceremony:

Ceremony Venue:

Order of Service printed? Yes [ ] No [ ]
Due to Funeral Director by:

Curtain Open [ ]
Curtain Closed [ ]
Interment Music [ ]

Notes

Name of Deceased:

Date of Birth: Date of Death:
Nature of passing:

Family visit: am/pm Day: Date:

Chief mourner:

Next of kin:

Address:

Postcode:

Email:

Phone:

Other family members/friends/chief executor:

Music

Wesley [ ]   Family Supplied [ ] Organ/piano [ ]

Obitus [ ]   Funeral Director [ ] Other [ ]

Processional

Title_____

Singer/Composer_____

Reflection

Title_____

Singer/Composer_____

Recessional

Title_____

Singer/Composer_____

Other Music

Hymns

Prayers or Blessings:

Readings/poems:

Tribute speakers:

Ritual/s:

Donations:

Funeral Tea:

Acknowledgements:

Ashes: Interment [ ] Scattering [ ]
Time:
Day and date:
Burial Site:

Funeral Director/Arranger:

[ ] Cremation

[ ] Burial

[ ] Memorial

Time:
Day:
Date of Ceremony:

Ceremony Venue:

Order of Service printed? Yes [ ] No [ ]
Due to Funeral Director by:

Curtain Open [ ]
Curtain Closed [ ]
Interment Music [ ]

Notes

Name of Deceased:

Date of Birth: Date of Death:
Nature of passing:

Family visit: am/pm Day: Date:

Chief mourner:

Next of kin:

Address:

Postcode:

Email:

Phone:

Other family members/friends/chief executor:

Music

Wesley [ ]   Family Supplied [ ] Organ/piano [   ]

Obitus [ ]   Funeral Director [ ] Other [ ]

Processional

Title_____

Singer/Composer_____

Reflection

Title_____

Singer/Composer_____

Recessional

Title_____

Singer/Composer_____

Other Music

Hymns

Prayers or Blessings:

Readings/poems:

Tribute speakers:

Ritual/s:

Donations:

Funeral Tea:

Acknowledgements:

Ashes: Interment [   ] Scattering [   ]
Time:
Day and date:
Burial Site:

Funeral Director/Arranger:

[ ] Cremation

[ ] Burial

[ ] Memorial

Time:
Day:
Date of Ceremony:

Ceremony Venue:

Order of Service printed? Yes [ ] No [ ]
Due to Funeral Director by:

Curtain Open [ ]
Curtain Closed [ ]
Interment Music [ ]

Notes

Name of Deceased:

Date of Birth: Date of Death:
Nature of passing:

Family visit: am/pm Day: Date:

Chief mourner:

Next of kin:

Address:

Postcode:

Email:

Phone:

Other family members/friends/chief executor:

Music

Wesley [ ]   Family Supplied [ ] Organ/piano [ ]

Obitus [ ]   Funeral Director [ ]   Other [ ]

Processional

Title_____

Singer/Composer_____

Reflection

Title_____

Singer/Composer_____

Recessional

Title_____

Singer/Composer_____

Other Music

Hymns

Prayers or Blessings:

Readings/poems:

Tribute speakers:

Ritual/s:

Donations:

Funeral Tea:

Acknowledgements:

Ashes: Interment [   ]   Scattering [   ]
Time:
Day and date:
Burial Site:

Funeral Director/Arranger:

[ ] Cremation

[ ] Burial

[ ] Memorial

Time:
Day:
Date of Ceremony:

Ceremony Venue:

Order of Service printed? Yes [ ] No [ ]
Due to Funeral Director by:

Curtain Open [ ]
Curtain Closed [ ]
Interment Music [ ]

Notes

Name of Deceased:

Date of Birth: Date of Death:
Nature of passing:

Family visit: am/pm Day: Date:

Chief mourner:

Next of kin:

Address:

Postcode:

Email:

Phone:

Other family members/friends/chief executor:

Music

Wesley [ ]   Family Supplied [ ] Organ/piano [ ]

Obitus [ ]   Funeral Director [ ]   Other [ ]

Processional

Title_____

Singer/Composer_____

Reflection

Title_____

Singer/Composer_____

Recessional

Title_____

Singer/Composer_____

Other Music

Hymns

Prayers or Blessings:

Readings/poems:

Tribute speakers:

Ritual/s:

Donations:

Funeral Tea:

Acknowledgements:

Ashes: Interment [   ] Scattering [   ]
Time:
Day and date:
Burial Site:

Funeral Director/Arranger:

[ ] Cremation

[ ] Burial

[ ] Memorial

Time:
Day:
Date of Ceremony:

Ceremony Venue:

Order of Service printed? Yes [ ] No [ ]
Due to Funeral Director by:

Curtain Open [ ]
Curtain Closed [ ]
Interment Music [ ]

Notes

Name of Deceased:

Date of Birth: Date of Death:
Nature of passing:

Family visit: am/pm Day: Date:

Chief mourner:

Next of kin:

Address:

Postcode:

Email:

Phone:

Other family members/friends/chief executor:

Music

Wesley [ ]   Family Supplied [ ] Organ/piano [ ]

Obitus [ ]   Funeral Director [ ]   Other [ ]

Processional

Title_____

Singer/Composer_____

Reflection

Title_____

Singer/Composer_____

Recessional

Title_____

Singer/Composer_____

Other Music

Hymns

Prayers or Blessings:

Readings/poems:

Tribute speakers:

Ritual/s:

Donations:

Funeral Tea:

Acknowledgements:

Ashes: Interment [ ] Scattering [ ]
Time:
Day and date:
Burial Site:

Funeral Director/Arranger:

[ ] Cremation

[ ] Burial

[ ] Memorial

Time:
Day:
Date of Ceremony:

Ceremony Venue:

Order of Service printed? Yes [ ] No [ ]
Due to Funeral Director by:

Curtain Open [ ]
Curtain Closed [ ]
Interment Music [ ]

Notes

Name of Deceased:

Date of Birth: Date of Death:
Nature of passing:

Family visit: am/pm Day: Date:

Chief mourner:

Next of kin:

Address:

Postcode:

Email:

Phone:

Other family members/friends/chief executor:

Music

Wesley [ ]   Family Supplied [ ] Organ/piano [   ]

Obitus   [ ]   Funeral Director [ ]   Other [ ]

Processional

Title_____

Singer/Composer_____

Reflection

Title_____

Singer/Composer_____

Recessional

Title_____

Singer/Composer_____

Other Music

Hymns

Prayers or Blessings:

Readings/poems:

Tribute speakers:

Ritual/s:

Donations:

Funeral Tea:

Acknowledgements:

Ashes: Interment [   ]   Scattering [   ]
Time:
Day and date:
Burial Site:

Funeral Director/Arranger:

[ ] Cremation

[ ] Burial

[ ] Memorial

Time:
Day:
Date of Ceremony:

Ceremony Venue:

Order of Service printed? Yes [ ] No [ ]
Due to Funeral Director by:

Curtain Open [ ]
Curtain Closed [ ]
Interment Music [ ]

Notes

Name of Deceased:

Date of Birth: Date of Death:
Nature of passing:

Family visit: am/pm Day: Date:

Chief mourner:

Next of kin:

Address:

Postcode:

Email:

Phone:

Other family members/friends/chief executor:

Music

Wesley [ ]   Family Supplied [ ] Organ/piano [   ]

Obitus [ ]   Funeral Director [ ]   Other [ ]

Processional

Title_____

Singer/Composer_____

Reflection

Title_____

Singer/Composer_____

Recessional

Title_____

Singer/Composer_____

Other Music

Hymns

Prayers or Blessings:

Readings/poems:

Tribute speakers:

Ritual/s:

Donations:

Funeral Tea:

Acknowledgements:

Ashes: Interment [   ]   Scattering [   ]
Time:
Day and date:
Burial Site:

Funeral Director/Arranger:

[ ] Cremation

[ ] Burial

[ ] Memorial

Time:
Day:
Date of Ceremony:

Ceremony Venue:

Order of Service printed? Yes [ ] No [ ]
Due to Funeral Director by:

Curtain Open [ ]
Curtain Closed [ ]
Interment Music [ ]

Notes

Name of Deceased:

Date of Birth: Date of Death:
Nature of passing:

Family visit: am/pm Day: Date:

Chief mourner:

Next of kin:

Address:

Postcode:

Email:

Phone:

Other family members/friends/chief executor:

Music

Wesley [ ]   Family Supplied [ ] Organ/piano [   ]

Obitus   [ ]   Funeral Director [ ]   Other [   ]

Processional

Title_____

Singer/Composer_____

Reflection

Title_____

Singer/Composer_____

Recessional

Title_____

Singer/Composer_____

Other Music

Hymns

Prayers or Blessings:

Readings/poems:

Tribute speakers:

Ritual/s:

Donations:

Funeral Tea:

Acknowledgements:

Ashes: Interment [   ]   Scattering [   ]
Time:
Day and date:
Burial Site:

Funeral Director/Arranger:

[ ] Cremation

[ ] Burial

[ ] Memorial

Time:
Day:
Date of Ceremony:

Ceremony Venue:

Order of Service printed? Yes [ ] No [ ]
Due to Funeral Director by:

Curtain Open [ ]
Curtain Closed [ ]
Interment Music [ ]

Notes

Name of Deceased:

Date of Birth: Date of Death:
Nature of passing:

Family visit: am/pm Day: Date:

Chief mourner:

Next of kin:

Address:

Postcode:

Email:

Phone:

Other family members/friends/chief executor:

Music

Wesley [ ]   Family Supplied [ ] Organ/piano [ ]

Obitus [ ]   Funeral Director [ ] Other [ ]

Processional

Title_____

Singer/Composer_____

Reflection

Title_____

Singer/Composer_____

Recessional

Title_____

Singer/Composer_____

Other Music

Hymns

Prayers or Blessings:

Readings/poems:

Tribute speakers:

Ritual/s:

Donations:

Funeral Tea:

Acknowledgements:

Ashes: Interment [ ] Scattering [ ]
Time:
Day and date:
Burial Site:

Funeral Director/Arranger:

[ ] Cremation

[ ] Burial

[ ] Memorial

Time:
Day:
Date of Ceremony:

Ceremony Venue:

Order of Service printed? Yes [ ] No [ ]
Due to Funeral Director by:

Curtain Open [ ]
Curtain Closed [ ]
Interment Music [ ]

Notes

Name of Deceased:

Date of Birth: Date of Death:
Nature of passing:

Family visit: am/pm Day: Date:

Chief mourner:

Next of kin:

Address:

Postcode:

Email:

Phone:

Other family members/friends/chief executor:

Music

Wesley [ ]   Family Supplied [ ] Organ/piano [   ]

Obitus [ ]   Funeral Director [ ] Other [ ]

Processional

Title_____

Singer/Composer_____

Reflection

Title_____

Singer/Composer_____

Recessional

Title_____

Singer/Composer_____

Other Music

Hymns

Prayers or Blessings:

Readings/poems:

Tribute speakers:

Ritual/s:

Donations:

Funeral Tea:

Acknowledgements:

Ashes: Interment [   ]   Scattering [   ]
Time:
Day and date:
Burial Site:

Funeral Director/Arranger:

[ ] Cremation

[ ] Burial

[ ] Memorial

Time:
Day:
Date of Ceremony:

Ceremony Venue:

Order of Service printed? Yes [ ] No [ ]
Due to Funeral Director by:

Curtain Open [ ]
Curtain Closed [ ]
Interment Music [ ]

Notes

Name of Deceased:

Date of Birth: Date of Death:
Nature of passing:

Family visit: am/pm Day: Date:

Chief mourner:

Next of kin:

Address:

Postcode:

Email:

Phone:

Other family members/friends/chief executor:

Music

Wesley [ ]   Family Supplied [ ] Organ/piano [ ]

Obitus   [ ]   Funeral Director [ ]   Other [ ]

Processional

Title_____

Singer/Composer_____

Reflection

Title_____

Singer/Composer_____

Recessional

Title_____

Singer/Composer_____

Other Music

Hymns

Prayers or Blessings:

Readings/poems:

Tribute speakers:

Ritual/s:

Donations:

Funeral Tea:

Acknowledgements:

Ashes: Interment [ ]   Scattering [ ]
Time:
Day and date:
Burial Site:

Funeral Director/Arranger:

[ ] Cremation

[ ] Burial

[ ] Memorial

Time:
Day:
Date of Ceremony:

Ceremony Venue:

Order of Service printed? Yes [ ] No [ ]
Due to Funeral Director by:

Curtain Open [ ]
Curtain Closed [ ]
Interment Music [ ]

Notes

Name of Deceased:

Date of Birth: Date of Death:
Nature of passing:

Family visit: am/pm Day: Date:

Chief mourner:

Next of kin:

Address:

Postcode:

Email:

Phone:

Other family members/friends/chief executor:

Music

Wesley [ ]   Family Supplied [ ] Organ/piano [   ]

Obitus [ ]   Funeral Director [ ]   Other [ ]

Processional

Title_____

Singer/Composer_____

Reflection

Title_____

Singer/Composer_____

Recessional

Title_____

Singer/Composer_____

Other Music

Hymns

Prayers or Blessings:

Readings/poems:

Tribute speakers:

Ritual/s:

Donations:

Funeral Tea:

Acknowledgements:

Ashes: Interment [   ] Scattering [   ]
Time:
Day and date:
Burial Site:

Notes

www.ingramcontent.com/pod-product-compliance
Lightning Source LLC
Chambersburg PA
CBHW080859090426
42734CB00032B/3000